Praise for Nehemiah Response

Nehemiah Response is a much-needed resource that is profound, accessible and challenging, yet comforting. By thoughtfully drawing from Scripture and authentically sharing his own Hurricane Katrina experience and ministry, Nelson Roth helps individuals and churches learn how to faithfully prepare for, make it through, and recover from crises.

—Jamie D. Aten, PhD, Assistant Professor of Psychology; Director of the Church Disaster Mental Health Project; Assistant Director of Health and Mental Health, Katrina Research Center at the University of Southern Mississippi; Co-editor of Spirituality and the Therapeutic Process (APA Books)

The devastation and destruction of Katrina was unprecedented, and so it demanded an unprecedented response by the faith community. Nelson Roth paints a clear picture of his church in action following Katrina as they provided a compassionate and intentional response to our nation's largest natural disaster at ground zero. *Nehemiah Response* is a must read for people of all faiths who are going through or wanting to prepare for the storms of life.

—John M. Hosey, MDiv, MS Coast
Interfaith Disaster Task Force

I found Nelson's story honest and inspiring. He provides a heartfelt, personal illustration of how hope carries us through suffering and tragedy. What the reader may find surprising is how well one can identify with Nehemiah's story and Hurricane Katrina survivors. Despite the uniqueness of their catastrophe, Nelson outlines in tangible ways how we can learn and grow from our own more ordinary struggles or personal tragedies.

—Josh Mathew, MD, Adult Psychiatrist,
Oaklawn Psychiatric Center, Inc, Goshen, Indiana

This book not only brings to life Pastor Nelson's experience with Hurricane Katrina and how his church responded; but also is instructive to us in our storms of life and how we respond to crisis. This is a very engaging and biblical read!

—Kevin King, Executive Director,
Mennonite Disaster Service, Akron, Pennsylvania

In Nelson Roth's book, *Nehemiah Response*, he addresses how to recover from a crisis with clarity, heart-felt compassion, and knowledge from one who has been through the storm. Not only does Nelson encourage church leadership by outlining a disaster preparedness plan, but he also speaks to individuals challenging personal spiritual growth. This is a must read book for men and women in leadership positions in order to prepare for any crisis. Being a well-prepared responder versus a reactor will make all the difference for those under your care and perhaps even more—for the cause of Christ.

—Candi Hallam, Christian Counselor
and Author of *Restore Always*

Nehemiah Response is a moving account of the rebuilding, restoration and renewal of a congregation after the onslaught of Hurricane Katrina. Nehemiah is revisited as this pastor and congregation, faced their losses, kept gathering to hear God's word and joined together to rebuild their lives and their life together. This is an excellent guide in "how to make it through a crisis."

—Marcus G. Smucker, PhD, professor emeritus
at the Associated Mennonite Biblical Seminary

If you're facing a challenge in ministry, Nelson Roth invites you to compare your challenge to the catastrophe of Katrina. The story of his church's recovery and revival, mixed with wisdom from Nehemiah's own rebuilding project, will inspire you with fresh hope for the future.

—Tom Harper, president of the
Society for Church Consulting and
publisher of ChurchCentral.com

NEHEMIAH
RESPONSE

CRISISRECOVERY
CRISISRECOVERY

NEHEMIAH
RESPONSE

CRISISRECOVERY

CRISISRECOVERY

CRISISRECOVERY

HOW TO MAKE
IT THROUGH
YOUR CRISIS

RECOVERY

RECOVERY

NELSON ROTH

COVERY

TATE PUBLISHING & *Enterprises*

Published by Tate Publishing & Enterprises, LLC
127 E. Trade Center Terrace | Mustang, Oklahoma 73064 USA
1.888.361.9473 | www.tatepublishing.com

Tate Publishing is committed to excellence in the publishing industry. The company reflects the philosophy established by the founders, based on Psalm 68:11,
"The Lord gave the word and great was the company of those who published it."

Book design copyright © 2009 by Tate Publishing, LLC. All rights reserved.
Cover design by Amber Gulilat
Interior design by Blake Brasor

Published in the United States of America

ISBN: 978-1-61566-225-8
1. Social Science, Disasters & Disaster Relief
2. Religion, Christian Life, Social Issues
09.09.14

Dedication

I want to thank my wife, Pam, who has been my ministry partner for over forty years; she is an inspiration to me. And I want to thank our three children, Rodney, Angela, and Andrea and their families. They continually encourage and pray for me.

Pam and I went through Hurricane Katrina and the crisis that followed. Rodney and Angela were first responders after the storm and made several trips to Mississippi to help in the recovery process. Andrea was supportive while starting her master's program in Chicago, which was what was right for her at that time. Without my family and God, this book would not have been possible.

Table of Contents

Acknowledgements

We are eternally grateful for all of the wonderful volunteers who partnered with us after Hurricane Katrina hit the Gulf Coast of Mississippi. For fourteen months, we had the privilege of hosting over 1,100 volunteers who lived at and worked out of our church. If it were not for those volunteers and the many others from faith-based organizations, I'm not sure where the entire Gulf Coast or Gulfhaven Mennonite Church would be today. Volunteers came from every region of the United States and Canada and are one of the main reasons we were able to make it through this major crisis.

As a result of their dedication and long hours of service, our church completed more than two hundred cleanup jobs and over eighty home-rebuilding projects. Each and every one of these projects is a remarkable story of someone helping and someone being helped.

The storm surge from Katrina may have been a twenty-five foot wall of water coming up from the Gulf, but the volunteers who came our way produced an even greater wave effect, bringing with them relief and rebuilding.

I am also grateful for the eldership team serving at our church during the time of Hurricane Katrina: David Bunn, Jay Burns, Scott Miller, Howard Walkinshaw, and Dave Weaver; plus all of the members and regular attendees of the church. As a novice to hurricanes, I am indebted to all of them for being a caring community that provided help for me and anyone else that came our way. Together, our congregation became a modern-day living-and-breathing body of Christ that rose up and met needs as they became known.

After being encouraged by a countless number of people to share our Hurricane Katrina experience, I've decided to write this book, *Nehemiah Response*. It's a memoir of our Hurricane Katrina stories, but it's much more than that. We also share principles we have learned and tested during our rebuilding process from the Bible in the book of Nehemiah. I just hope that I am able to convey to you the power of this storm, what it is like to *ride a storm out*, and our long but blessed journey of rebuilding.

Not every story can be told because that would add up to a stack of newspapers or television news scripts much higher than the storm surge itself. If you experienced Katrina either as a resident or volunteer, I have included several blank pages at the end of the book to list and record your remembrances. Hopefully, someday we can meet and share those stories as well.

How to Use
This Book

Nehemiah Response is more than a memoir of Hurricane Katrina experiences, it is a book designed to help some-one through a crisis. If you are facing a difficult time in your life, the principles in this book may be exactly what you need to help you through and to give you a sense of direction and hope.

Nehemiah Response has been laid out so that a church could develop a disaster response ministry. You may also use the book as a Bible study with a small group, in an adult Bible class, or as a personal study.

In Appendix I of *Nehemiah Response*, you will find a section specifically designed to help churches and ministries with a disaster preparedness plan and how to develop a disaster response ministry. In this section you will find some great resources and suggestions as you develop a team to put together your contingency plan. If a disaster came your way, would you be prepared? Learn how to sustain yourself during an emergency and to be ready to seize ministry opportunities that follow.

In Appendix II, the personal study guide, you will find questions to stimulate your thinking for each chapter in the book and Website links to corresponding audio messages. If you choose to follow the layout of the book, you can plan to take at least twelve weeks to study the book, *Nehemiah Response*.

Introduction

Have you ever sat through a movie where the events seemed unreal? Think about the last time you saw a movie about a catastrophic event or perhaps you are an avid sci-fi fan. There it is on the big screen ... the world is falling apart from some natural disaster, a ship is sinking or a plane is crashing. Or worse than that, some biological warfare has been released and everything in the town is burning up, and those that inhabit the city are evacuating to escape the destruction. Well, that is exactly how I felt as the days progressed after Hurricane Katrina. Leading up to that event, things were going pretty well, and it was great living on the Mississippi Gulf Coast.

As a matter of fact, I have a vivid memory of Saturday, August 27, 2005. The sun was shining; the sky was a brilliant blue. Hummingbirds were zipping around our feeders, and a gentle tropical breeze was coming in from the Gulf—all adding up to a pretty incredible day in south Mississippi. The gorgeous weather, along with it being Saturday, was the kind of day that brings folks together on their front porches in Mississippi—spending a little time in a rocking chair, sipping sweet tea and talking about things in their lives.

If it wasn't for the weather technology, we would have had no idea about what was going to happen to us. There were no visible signs that we would soon be hustling to cover the windows of our home with plywood. It wasn't until early Sunday morning, when we realized that south Mississippi would be a direct target on Hurricane Katrina's path.

I got up early that Sunday morning as usual to pray and put finishing touches on the message for our worship service. Typically, I would not turn on the television on Sunday morning, but on August 28, 2005, I did. When we went to bed on Saturday evening, both Katrina's intensity and target were uncertain, so I wanted to check on the latest projected path for Hurricane Katrina. When I saw the weather map on our local station and heard the reporter saying the winds had intensified and its course was more certain, I got chills from the realization that we were definitely going to experience this monstrous storm.

At 5:00 a.m., I called the leaders of the church with the latest information. Together, we decided that it would be best to cancel our Sunday morning services. It was becoming increasingly apparent that it was time to either *get out* or *get ready*. Little did we know, at that time, the importance of being prepared until we were faced with what turned out to be our nation's worst natural disaster.

Have you ever noticed that seems to be the way we get hit with a disaster? It's quiet and beautiful *just before the storm*. Sometimes a disaster hits us by surprise. In some cases, there may be an advanced warning, but either way—surprise or warning—we still get hit. Your disaster may not be a hurricane. Your disaster may be financial, relational, or something else, but there is one common denominator with all disasters—there will be a crisis to follow.

What Do You Do When Something Bad Strikes?

Those who survived the exile and are back in the province are in great trouble and disgrace. The wall of Jerusalem is broken down, and its gates have been burned with fire.

Nehemiah 1:3

August 29, 2005, was the longest day I've ever experienced in my life, and I don't mind admitting that during that day, I was afraid. On that day, my wife, Pam, and I rode out Hurricane Katrina in our home, nine miles north of the Mississippi Gulf Coast.

Katrina has impacted the lives of all of us who live along the Mississippi Gulf Coast. Jeff Lawson of WLOX, our south Mississippi television station, began a Hurricane Katrina documentary by saying,

It was a storm that hit with such force and such fury. It caused south Mississippians to rethink the very standard by which they measure hurricanes. On August 28, 2005, that standard was Hurricane Camille, a legendary 1969 storm that devastated the area. One day later, the destruction from Camille would pale in comparison. What people saw was astounding. It seemed impossible, and to some unthinkable, that south Mississippi could have a hurricane with more destructive power and more deadly force than Hurricane Camille; but that's exactly what happened on August 29, 2005. ... one of nature's greatest forces, a monster hurricane named Katrina, would change our vibrant community for evermore.[1]

Events, landmarks, and countless memories of the Gulf Coast are talked about now in terms of either the way it was before, or more often, how it is since Hurricane Katrina.

Something Bad Strikes

At the time of Katrina, my wife, Pam, and I had lived in south Mississippi for only a year and a half. A church in Gulfport had called me to serve as their lead pastor. As first-time Coastal residents, we were settling in and having the time of our lives. Being new to the area, we were experiencing the culture and learning the local colloquialisms, which was a delight.

We had been in the ministry for over thirty-five years. We had served in five churches—mostly in the Midwest. God's divine leading brought us to the South and a church made up of special folks. Almost instantly, there was a connection and a reciprocal love—something I believe we all needed at that time. However, the one thing this loving congregation forgot to share with me was the fact that there is such a thing as *hurricane season* along the Gulf Coast. Yes, it is true the topic of hurricanes never came up even one time. I guess that wasn't something they wanted to put in their brochure.

In our first months on the Gulf Coast, this Midwestern pastor did something he had never experienced before—he secured plywood boards to the windows of his home three times. The third time was Hurricane Katrina. So what do you do when something bad strikes?

In our situation, we secured our windows and doors with plywood, stocked up on water and nonperishable items, stored water in the washing machine and our two bathtubs. Oh yes, and we purchased a supply of batteries. We prepared the best we could in the short amount of time we had before the hurricane was predicted to strike. Then, on Sunday evening, we *hunkered down* just as we had done many times before during a snow storm in the Midwest. Only this time, we waited anxiously for something we had never experienced before—the arrival of a hurricane, not an ordinary hurricane but Hurricane Katrina.

Riding Out the Storm

According to reports, Katrina made landfall in Mississippi as a Category 3 hurricane at 7:00 on Monday morning, August 29, 2005; however, the electricity in our area of the city was out by 5:30 a.m. The house was dark, and the atmosphere outside was eerie. It wasn't long until sustaining winds rose from seventy miles per hour to 120 miles per hour, with gusts of 135 miles per hour. During that period of time, the sound of relentless wind was chilling, and it seemed as though the storm would never end.

> The Gulf Coast of Mississippi suffered massive damage...leaving 238 people dead, sixty-seven missing, and billions of dollars in damage: bridges, barges, boats, piers, houses and cars were washed inland. After making a brief initial landfall in Louisiana, Katrina had made its final landfall near the state line, and the eyewall passed over the cities of Bay St. Louis and Waveland as a Category 3 hurricane with sustained winds of 120 mph (195 km/h). Katrina's powerful right-front quadrant passed over the west and central Mississippi Coast, causing a powerful twenty-seven foot (8.2 m) storm surge, which penetrated six miles (10 km) inland in many areas and up to twelve miles (20 km) inland along bays and rivers; in some areas, the surge crossed Interstate 10 for several miles.[2]

In preparation for the storm, we were told about the tornadoes that spin out of the continuous hurricane-force winds. Within the first hour, we began to hear a sound I'd never heard before—the sound of a freight train barreling toward our house. It wasn't long before I realized that was the sound of a tornado. Tornados were above our roof, zipping through our yard, and swirling the tops of trees out of control. Our house was already cracking from the relentless hurricane winds; and now, we had the added dynamic of listening to at least eight tornados dancing around our property. At one time during the storm, I thought, *Maybe we will survive the hurricane winds, but what if one of the tornados targets our house?*

Most of the homes along the Gulf Coast do not have basements. Our home, like most, was built on a concrete slab. No basement means no shelter to go to, so what do you do to protect yourself from the storm? Being rookies to the whole hurricane experience, we chose to go to a center hallway in our one-story home. We had a small television—that became useless as soon as we lost electricity, flashlights, our cell phones, a portable radio, granola bars, and bottled water.

As the sound of the tornados intensified, I became increasingly apprehensive about the structure of our home. Our home has cathedral ceilings in the main part of the house, and by this time, the sound of the support beams being tested by the increasing winds was a source of concern. Added to the sound of the wind, ever so often, we could hear something being thrown against our house. The good thing is, we had covered all of the windows and doors to protect us from the possibility of flying glass. On the downside of that, we could not see what was being thrust against our house. There was one ray of hope … literally; a ray of light was able to come in through an uncovered arched window above our front door.

At one point, I hurried out to the garage to get a stepladder tall enough to reach the top of the door. This would provide a way for us to see what was happening outside. The only thing was, I forgot that we had created a vacuum in our house by sealing everything up so tightly. So when I opened the door from the house to the garage, the forceful winds outside pressed against the garage door—almost pushing the overhead door completely in. When I turned to go back into the house, I saw Pam standing in the doorway with the most concerned look on her face. She had heard the noise in the garage and thought that the door was going to be blown off of its track; leaving me and the contents of our garage open and vulnerable to the winds of the storm.

Being a man who by nature thinks in terms of systems and solutions, I decided to add something to our campsite in our hallway. I had pondered what would be the most effective solution. So with the next big *cracking sound*, I moved one of our couches into the hallway, flipped it over and strengthened our new fortress. It was under that couch, with a flashlight that Pam and I spent the remainder of the next seven hours talking and praying.

So what can you do when you are about to be hit by a storm? You prepare as best you can for the duration of the storm, and you ride it out.

Seeking Help Beyond Yourself

Having the Lord with us as our provider and protector was essential. Today, we joke about crawling under the couch and staying in those cramped conditions for seven hours, but the truth is we were scared—scared about the decision we had made to stay in our home, scared that the winds or a tornado would bring the structure of our house down, and most of all, scared that we may never see or talk to our family again. However, we are so grateful that we have a relationship with the God of creation. He is the one that kept us safe. His provision and protection is the key to our Hurricane Katrina experience. Without that connection—the lifeline to a living God, I'm not sure how we would have handled this situation. Isn't it wonderful to know that he makes these provisions not only for us, but for everyone who has invited him to become their Lord and Savior? Going through a storm—experiencing his presence—that's the most incredible thing.

Likewise, Nehemiah sought help beyond himself. Through the remainder of this book, we will be looking at principles in the Bible from the book of Nehemiah. You will discover that those same principles are transferable to your situation. However, for those principles to fully work it is essential that you know the God of the principles. The first step is to open your heart and invite the Lord not only into your disaster, but into your life. "He who has the Son has life; he who does not have the Son of God does not have life" (1 John 5:12). I'm a preacher, but I don't want to preach to you. I'm merely encouraging you to highly consider this step—to invite the Lord to become your Savior, if you do not already know him personally. Sometimes things just happen; a disaster may come to bring you to this important place. I truly believe that "…in all things God works for the good of those who love him…" (Romans 8:28).

In Nehemiah chapter one, the layman Nehemiah discovered the full extent of the disaster he was about to face. Gripped with the news, he responded, "When I heard these things, I sat down and wept" (1:4). Then he prayed, "O Lord, God of heaven, the great and awesome God, who keeps his covenant of love..." (1:5). In the same way, your disaster may make you so weak at the knees that you have to sit down and cry. Will you include God in your life and experience his promise of love for you?

Making a Right Response in Your Disaster

As far as God is concerned, there are usually two responses that people take when faced with a disaster. We will run to him, or we will run from him. It's a choice we make. We could go as far as blaming God for what happened, or we can choose to find him because of the disaster. Nehemiah begins his prayer with praise. He calls God *awesome*. I want to challenge you to discover God in a deeper way because of your disaster.

Next, Nehemiah models the character trait of responsibility in his prayer—he repents. Too often, we cringe at the word repentance. The fact is, repentance is basically being honest about what we've done wrong and purposing with God's help to make a dramatic change. Nehemiah goes on to say, "I confess" (1:6). And then he adds, "We have acted very wickedly toward you [God]. We have not obeyed the commands" (1:7).

Are you the cause of a disaster in your life, or do you feel like you are the victim of the disaster? This is an interesting question. Either way, when we act responsibly, we can make some important changes that have been revealed by our disaster and come through it as a better person by gaining valuable life lessons.

Most of us can remember where we were on September 11, 2001. The terrorist attack of 9/11 has impacted us all. This disaster brought with it a whole new level of fear for Americans, but it also brought with it changes that have been good for the security of our country. If you've flown lately, the precautions taken in getting through security are constant reminders.

Here's something else interesting that is related to how the terrorist attacks affected us. A George Barna study provides observations, from data gathered, in a report five years after 9/11:

> The study shows that despite an intense surge in religious activity and expression in the weeks immediately following 9/11 the faith of Americans is virtually indistinguishable today compared to pre-attack conditions.[3]

The Barna study goes on to say,

> In the immediate aftermath of the attacks, half of all Americans said their faith helped them cope with the shock and uncertainty. The change most widely reported was a significant spike in church attendance, with some churches experiencing more than double their normal crowd on the Sunday after the shocking event. However, by the time January 2002 rolled around, churchgoing was back to pre-attack levels, and has remained consistent in the five years since.
>
> Other religious behaviors, if they were affected at all, found equilibrium even more quickly. As of October 2001, Americans' engagement in Bible reading and prayer was no different than pre-attack levels and has been essentially consistent from that point on.[4]

The director of the study, David Kinnaman, said,

Many Christian leaders predicted that terrorism on U.S. soil would catalyze a spiritual awakening in the country. The first few weeks were promising. But people quickly returned to their standard, faith-as-usual lives: within a month, most of their spiritual fervor was gone. Within 90 days, surprisingly few people were pursuing important questions about faith and spirituality.[5]

As unbelievable as this may seem, even a major catastrophe like the terrorist attacks on the Twin Towers and the Pentagon has not changed most Americans spiritually. It seems as though the response was to restore continuity and comfort as quickly as possible without making an effort to grow morally or spiritually.

Seeking to find a *comfortable place* again seems to be one response to a disaster. Let me ask you a direct question: "Would it be worth it to take an alternative route through the crisis and let the disaster be used for God's perfecting work in you?"

For us, the decision had already been made—we were going through the storm. Monday, August 29, 2005, was a long, stressful day, and it wasn't until 5:00 p.m. that we opened the front door of our home and ventured outside. What we saw was unbelievable. Trees were fallen everywhere. Roofs were peeled back. A home nearby was leveled by a tornado. Although our house had roof damage and a gable had been blown out, exposing our attic, the structure was still standing and the house was livable. We were so thankful to be alive, but we had no idea at that time the extent of the devastation along the Mississippi Gulf Coast.

You've survived your disaster, what's next? If you

have chosen to run *to* and not *from* God, what does he have to say? Does God have a plan in mind? Now is the best time to consider what might be *God's idea* for you as a result of your disaster. We'll consider more about this as we begin the next chapter.

So, Is There a Plan for Me in All of This?

For my thoughts are not your thoughts, neither are your ways my ways, declares the Lord. As the heavens are higher than the earth, so are my ways higher than your ways and my thoughts than your thoughts.

Isaiah 55:8–9

Though we had storm damage to contend with, Pam and I felt fortunate because we still had a house to live in. During the first days after Hurricane Katrina, we discovered that no one was left untouched. Some homes were completely washed out into the Gulf, while others were smashed to the ground. Homeowners with a house that was still standing would have to deal with wind and water damage: repairing the roof, shoveling out silt and sand, and sorting through personal belongings. The unfortunate thing about a disaster is that it never comes alone. If there is a disaster, you can almost always count on dealing with a crisis in some form.

Seeing Your Situation From God's Perspective

Early on, I felt like we were on a Lewis and Clark adventure of sorts. We found ourselves on a path we'd never walked before—a place where needs and solutions were discovered as we moved forward. Responding to our nation's worst natural disaster has been a daunting challenge. Looking back, I am amazed that we have come so far, yet there are still challenges that we face daily.

Our church building was compromised by the storm, we had to put a plan into place to not only minister to the needs of the congregation, but restore the church building. Many of our members not only had their homes to deal with, but some of them worked their jobs seven days a week, twelve and fourteen hours a day. In an effort to lessen the pressure on our people, the church leadership decided that it would be best to cancel all church activity except for our Sunday morning worship service. Relief from the disaster became our focus, but gathering to worship and hear from the Word was essential.

It was early in the fall of 2005 when I decided to preach through the book of Nehemiah. Everyone was seeking answers and needing encouragement. We have come to realize that the Lord had a plan when he led me to study and preach from the book of Nehemiah.

It is obvious to me now that we were living out our Nehemiah response during this difficult time of crisis. So, how do you put a plan together when the needs are overwhelming?

Out of our crisis, we have learned some very valuable lessons. Though we were without a map on this Lewis and Clark adventure, we had the most important tool—the Word of God. Nehemiah was a source of encouragement to us. The words seemed to jump out of the book to provide light to our path. In the book of Nehemiah, we found an example to follow and principles to help with daily decisions and actions. Although we did not call it a *Nehemiah Response* at the time, looking back we see that's what happened.

One of the initial things we learned from the book of Nehemiah was *action is not necessarily the first response*. When Nehemiah heard of the destruction in Jerusalem, he pondered and prayed. He took time to discover what God may be doing. He attempted to see his situation from God's perspective. A quick *action* can just be a *reaction* to what is going on. Nehemiah's first response was to seek out God and see the problem from his perspective. Nehemiah did this before the king released him to go to Jerusalem (2:7), and when he got there, Nehemiah took time again to survey the site (2:11–12). Staying in step with God and joining him is imperative. Like Nehemiah, we learned that our first response wasn't to make plans; but to begin to realize that God had a plan, a purpose, and a reason for us as a result of this disaster.

Taking Time to Assess Needs

Our first challenge after Katrina was to connect with all of the member families in our church. We were a smaller congregation—a total of 106 families, and yet it took eleven days to complete the process. Since Katrina had taken a 125-mile wide swath of land between Mobile and New Orleans, we had major obstacles to overcome. Some people had stayed in their homes, while others had evacuated all over the country; therefore, making connections with others seemed impossible and primitive, at best. Prior to Hurricane Katrina, we didn't have a preparedness communication plan; so, facing the challenge to communicate with our church body opened our eyes to areas where we needed to be better prepared for a crisis.

On the eleventh day, one of our members, Rose Fletcher, was checked off the list. Rose was the last person that we needed to contact. With everyone accounted for, our immediate response was one of relief. Praise God, there had been no casualties out of the folks from our church.

No doubt, there would have been some casualties had some of our people not evacuated. Several members lived in apartments where the buildings were completely destroyed and where casualties had taken place. Others lived close by where a casualty took place. We had members who had eight feet of water in their homes. The most was twenty-seven feet. Some members of our congregation had five feet and others had several inches. Water damage or no water damage everyone had trees on the ground and roofs or gables to repair on their homes.

Not only was it a challenge to connect with everyone in our congregation, it was almost impossible to connect with our family in Illinois. Two days passed before I had miraculously connected with my dad. I had tried several times to call out to our family on my cell phone; but unfortunately, there was never a connection. Then one time, I dialed his number and the phone began to ring. In amazement, I just stood there, and then I heard…"Hello." It was my dad's voice. I was shocked that we finally connected. Immediately, my dad began to express our family's concerns for our wellbeing. It was a short conversation that day, but we were able to relay the message that we were alive and doing as well as could be expected.

Obtaining Basic Essentials for Survival

Before the end of the first week, two of our three children, Rodney and Angela, had organized a supply run from Illinois to Mississippi. They purchased supplies, and then along with two friends from our previous church, Jason Morris and Joe Knoerle, loaded a truck down with toiletries, cleaning supplies, and nonperishable goods for the members of our church. On that trip, our children also brought much-needed gasoline in multiple five-gallon gas cans.

The trip was necessary but dangerous. What a lot of people do not realize is that most of the state was affected by Hurricane Katrina. After the eye of the storm passed over the Waveland-Bay St. Louis area, the storm continued on a northeastern track up the state of Mississippi.

Most of the state did not have power, and debris and power lines had not been completely removed from the roads. One of the major dilemmas for traveling was the fact that many of the gas stations were closed in the state. In a conversation with a friend who works for Homeland Security, we were warned that caravans were being ambushed and pirated. People were carrying guns, and they were not afraid to use them.

To this day, I am brought to tears when I think of how our children put themselves in harm's way to be a servant of Christ to our congregation. We knew that they were arriving the Sunday following Katrina, but we did not know the exact time of their arrival. It was midway through the worship service when we heard the church doors swing open. People began to turn around. I was up front leading our congregation in a time of sharing our Katrina experiences, so I saw them come in. But as Pam turned around, she saw them standing there, and she began to cry. What an answer to prayer to see our children safe and to be united with them once again.

Although there are many stories of how God provided that first week, one of my favorite stories is the one our son, Rod, told about that trip down from Illinois. He told us how the team had prayed to be surrounded by angels for safety on the trip and that they would be able to find gasoline along the way. The Lord had been faithful as they traveled. As they approached the Gulf Coast, they needed to fill up with gasoline for the last time to ensure that they would have enough gasoline to finish the trip to Gulfport and to begin their return trip home to Illinois. Fortunately, they were able to find a gas station north of Jackson, Mississippi, that was operating. While filling the tank to the truck, our son said the team became uneasy, and their concerns about being robbed were becoming heightened. The team decided to pray, and when they were finished, out of nowhere appeared an entourage of official government vehicles going south to Highway 49. Like a child standing in amazement at a parade, they watched the vehicles with their flashing lights drive past them one by one. And then, there was a hesitation in the traffic, so quickly they maneuvered into the fifty-car caravan. Here's the most unbelievable part of this story: the caravan delivered their truck filled with supplies from Jackson to Gulfport just four miles from where the church is located. Our son said, "It was as though the Lord had placed a band of angels around them."

Does God surround us with angels? I believe he does, and I also believe that the Lord surrounds us with the help we need during a crisis. He has a plan!

Help From Others

Early on in the book of Nehemiah, we find Nehemiah being joined by others. In chapter one, when Nehemiah prayed in response to the condition of Jerusalem, he evidently had some prayer partners. "O Lord, let your ear be attentive to the prayer of this your servant and to the prayer of your servants who delight in revering your name" (1:11). When Nehemiah arrived in Jerusalem, before he announced his plan to rebuild publicly, he surveyed the city with others. He says in the second chapter, "I set out during the night with a few men" (2:12).

Have you noticed how a crisis seems to drive us

inward? All the emotions of hurt, confusion, uncertainty, and sadness make it hard to open up and reach out; let alone get started with what needs to be done. I am convinced that this is the point where we need at least one friend. Someone we can trust. Someone we will allow to get close to us after we've been through the disaster.

Three days after Katrina, people were not able to come in or out of the storm-torn area where we lived; however, two men came to my home—J. D. Landis, a pastor friend from Mobile, Alabama, and Kevin King, the director of Mennonite Disaster Service (MDS), our denomination's disaster agency. Fortunately, Kevin was able to fly into Mobile. Once in Mobile, Kevin and J. D. departed for Gulfport. Somehow, in the midst of blocked and barricaded roads, those two men were able to reach their destination—our home.

J. D. tells of the miraculous way we connected that day by saying,

> As I remember it, Kevin and I set out for Gulfport hoping to connect with Nelson and Pam. The problem was that I knew only generally where they lived and had no idea how to find them. Of course, there was the cell phone number that I had. Several times I tried to call, but cell phones were not working. I remember traveling north on Hwy 49, and I suggested to Kevin that we try one more time. That time it worked, and we got through to them. As I recall, it was the only time the cell phone worked that day. And amazingly, it worked just long enough for us to connect and get directions to the Roth's home. As things turned out, we were just a few miles from their home. We

believed God was leading the way, but at the same time, I remember thinking that the trip could be a total loss, if we could not find them. It was another affirmation that God was in the storm and in the aftermath. He never leaves us!

When J. D. and Kevin arrived, I was outside aimlessly picking up shingles and other debris, piling it up along the curb of our street. The weather was unbearable after Hurricane Katrina. It was hot and humid, and it did not take long to become uncomfortable. Although our house wasn't any cooler, we decided to go inside to sit down and talk about what might be next. There weren't a lot of answers that day about what to do, but news from the outside was welcomed. As we sat and talked in our living room, we all agreed that it was nothing short of a miracle that they were able to get to us. That visit was exactly what we needed to renew our hope and to see that God had a plan.

Because we did not have electricity, we were unable to hear or see any of the news stories about the storm and the damage it had caused. We had lost all means of communication with the outside world. So, it wasn't until J. D. and Kevin's visit that we realized we were in the middle of what the news media was now calling the *nation's worst natural disaster*. We couldn't believe what we were hearing. It almost felt like we were in some sci-fi movie and we had lost touch with all reality. The only thing that gave us a connection to the words that we were hearing was the sound of military planes flying day and night over our house bringing in supplies. We mentioned to the men that we had felt like we were in a war zone or a third-world country.

Several days after J. D. and Kevin's visit, we saw the front page headline in our daily *Sun Herald Newspaper*, from the day after the storm—"Our Tsunami." It was a quote from Biloxi's mayor A. J. Holloway and appeared in the paper dated Tuesday, August 30, 2005. The headline's byline was "At least fifty die in a storm as fearsome as Camille."[6] Being starved for information, we consumed the week-old news in the story and the horrific pictures on the cover page. There was so much more to learn, and our circle of information was increasing. We were still feeling the isolation caused by Katrina; however, it was becoming less with each day.

Isolation, whether it's done to us—like in our case—or if we do it to ourselves, is something to get beyond early on. Often, we need somebody else to begin to speak good news to us and to bring us comfort and hope. Who do you have right now in your life that you can trust and talk with openly?

Getting Started with the Obvious

The Monday after Katrina, the first group of volunteers arrived, and we were thrust into the relief and cleanup phase of restoring the homes of our neighbors, parishioners, and our church. Even now, it is hard to express how blessed we felt by the folks who drove halfway across the country to help us in our time of need. It didn't take long to discover that God had a plan and we were not alone in our crisis.

For us, hope began to take form with some of the first work crews. One of those crews was led by a man named John Beiler. John and his crew of twenty men came to help with clean up at the church and at homes around our area. They came with a loaded eighteen-wheeler carrying 80,000 pounds of skid loaders, chain saws, tools, gasoline, diesel fuel, and food. Jokingly, we would say that most of that 80,000 pounds was home-cooked meals and homemade pies, rolls, and pastries.

Talking about food … being without electricity for eight or nine days meant that we had not had a home-cooked meal for over a week, so when we sat down to eat a meal with these twenty men, it was like sitting down at a banquet table. Although the *spread* was especially prepared in advance by the hands of their wives and the table was filled with friends and family members from Pennsylvania, we felt an immediate acceptance at the table.

These wonderful people were Amish; Amish men who began preparing for the trip as soon as they heard that Hurricane Katrina had made landfall. These first responders were willing and ready to go. They were just waiting to hear where their destination was. John's crew was self-contained and experienced. Those men were ready to meet the challenges set before them. Suddenly, what had seemed impossible to us began to have possibilities. This was both good news and a ray of hope.

And hope is exactly what we needed during those first weeks. At that time, we were simply living in the moment, surviving one day at a time. Little did I know then that we would be doing relief and rebuilding work for the next fourteen months. Thank God for these twenty men who paved the way for the 1,100 plus volunteers that came to help with relief and rebuilding work out of our church.

As I write this, I have to reflect back to the Saturday before John and his group arrived. I was feeling overwhelmed. We still did not have electricity at our home; however, the electricity and phone service had just been restored at the church. Now that it was possible to communicate with people, I decided that the fastest means of communication to a large number of people would be by E-mail. So I logged into my E-mail and found that my inbox was filled with messages from friends out of state who said things like this:

"How are you?"
"What do you need?"
"How can we help?"
"When can we come?"

These messages from family and friends were incredible and overwhelming!

Without hesitation, I mentioned to some folks from our church that I was feeling overwhelmed and that we needed to begin putting a plan together if we were going to be able to accomplish the insurmountable task before us. At that time, I knew *what* we needed, but I wasn't sure *how* we were going to be able to fulfill all of the needs before us. This was a big task, and it would take a team of people with strong administrative and organizational skills. We needed someone to assess needs, organize jobs at worksites, schedule and coordinate volunteer crews, and help with distribution of supplies. In passing, I mentioned the need to Pam, and before I knew it, an initial team of volunteers from our congregation had been called and assembled. Within hours, six of us—Debbie Sullivan, Brenda (Plaice) Deen, Lisa

Boone, Ginger Bunn, Pam, and I—were creating a plan and putting systems in place to host volunteer teams and meet the needs of our congregation.

That story reiterates how important it is to have the right team of people around you during a crisis. Looking back, it is also a testimony to the dedicated people in our congregation who were willing to use their talents and gifts to serve. The church is a living organism that's made up of people, and its members have gifts through which God works. A healthy response can help a local church sustain itself during an emergency and then position itself to seize ministry opportunities that follow.

Are you are in a crisis? Look to God; see it from his perspective. Discover what God may be doing in your situation. Do your best to get in step with him. Also, look around and be open to receive what someone close by may have to offer to help you where you're at right now. My prayer is that you might be blessed in your own *Nehemiah response.*

Things seemed to be coming together. We didn't have the whole thing planned out, but we were beginning to see God's plan for us. The plan, simply stated, was that we were to be involved in disaster relief and rebuilding after Katrina. All the details were yet to come, but first, we needed to wrap our minds around this.

So, putting the details aside, what is God's plan or his idea for you because of your crisis? Once you have nailed that down, you can begin to think about the details. So how does a plan come together? How do you make decisions and put a plan together when your mind is still reeling from what you've gone through? Let's take that step in chapter three.

How Do You Put a Plan Together?

"…the gracious hand of my God was upon me."
"Then I said to them, 'You see the trouble we are
in: Jerusalem lies in ruins, and its gates have been
burned with fire. Come, let us rebuild the wall of
Jerusalem, and we will no longer be in disgrace.' I
also told them about the gracious hand of my God
upon me and what the king had said to me."

Nehemiah 2:8, 17–18

In the mid-1980s, a popular television program was
called *The A-Team*. In each episode, the team found
themselves in challenging situations. Prior to the team's
critical mission, they would always say—what became
the show's famous line, "I love it when a plan comes
together."

Just like in the episodes of the A-Team, the next part of moving through a crisis is the development of a plan. Once we've resolved that God has a plan, it's our job to begin making plans as we continue to look to him. And you may not be surprised, but Nehemiah can help us here, too.

The day of opportunity came for Nehemiah to share his heart with the king. Nehemiah, a captive of Babylon, was employed as the cupbearer for King Artaxerxes (2:1) in the citadel of Susa (1:1) about eight hundred miles to the east of Jerusalem. Nehemiah had been praying for over one hundred days (1:1 "month of Kislev," 2:1 "month of Nisan"), and God orchestrated a right-time/right-place moment.

The king said, "What is it you want?" (2:4)

Nehemiah responded, "If it pleases the king and if your servant has found favor in his sight, let him send me to the city in Judah where my fathers are buried so that I can rebuild it" (2:5).

The door of opportunity was now open, and as the conversation continued, he was able to share the plan that had come together.

Nehemiah knew what to ask for because he had been spending time with God learning his plan for the rebuilding of the wall. He also had been praying with a few other people along the same lines. Nehemiah asked to be sent; and it was granted to him. Because Nehemiah had been praying and planning, he knew what he needed to get started. Nehemiah asked for specific provisions and protection, and the king gave it to him. Nehemiah knew he was in step with God's plan,

"...because the gracious hand of my God was upon me, the king granted my requests" (2:8).

For us, the plan was coming together, and the details to start relief and recovery work began to fall into place. Some of the first things you do after a disaster are merely temporary *stopgap* measures, and the permanent solutions will follow. We experienced this while repairing roofs that had been damaged by the winds of Katrina.

Early on, we learned that blue tarps on roofs don't last long. The tarps met an immediate need; however, it was a temporary fix. Not too far into the relief work, a volunteer team of workers helping our church was called out to an emergency with several homes that had tarps blowing off in a thunderstorm. I was part of that group. My task was to get up on the roof in the wind and rain in an attempt to secure the tarp. Along with another worker, we grabbed the two loose corners of the tarp. I sat on the top ridge while hanging on to the blue tarp blowing in the wind like a sail. I remember hanging on for dear life. After much struggle, we finally got that blue tarp secured.

Our relief response happened in three phases. Early on, it was more *reactive* because there were urgent needs to be met. At first, people had trees on their homes and across their driveways that needed to be removed. Roofs had holes in them, so people needed blue tarps to keep their house dry. Moving forward, we tried to sense how God was leading in order to become *proactive* in our efforts.

It was amazing to watch the Lord bring the right people to move the project forward. He always provided the needed labor for our relief work projects. Phase I was ten weeks of cleanup work. Work crews helped our church members and neighbors who lived in a ten-mile radius of the church building. In December, Phase II, a rebuilding phase for church members and regular attendees began. We also had a church building that needed a lot of work, and that began the following March. Phase III was a rebuilding outreach.

During those first ten weeks of cleanup, we set a ten-mile radius around our church as a target area for our volunteers to work in. We wanted to include all of our church body, so our church members and regular attendees were included in the relief efforts wherever they lived. We then established work cards for people to request help for cleanup projects. On Sundays, at worship services and throughout the week, people would fill out a work card listing their address and the type of cleanup work they needed help with. It didn't take long for the word to spread that our church was officially doing relief work.

Finally, it felt like we had direction. We had some sense of where we were going and what we were going to do. We were experiencing our God-moments when plans miraculously came together. The book of Nehemiah sheds some light on the important aspects of the planning process.

Rest Isn't Optional

Here's what happened for Nehemiah. When Nehemiah first arrived in Jerusalem, he rested three days. I know what you're thinking: *You've got to be kidding, right? Are you saying that Nehemiah arrived on the scene and he didn't do anything?* Granted, there was so much to do; however, they had just completed an eight hundred-mile

How Do You Put a Plan Together?

journey that probably took around four months. The trip was exhausting. They rested, which was the most important thing that was needed at the time. With this, we can learn the importance of balance in our lives. But there's so much to do, we've got to get a move on.

Have you noticed how the days go by so quickly? We live in a world where everyone is moving at a break-neck pace. We're so *busy* oriented. And in the middle of our busyness, it would do us good to consider what evidently Nehemiah understood. He was worn out from his long journey to Jerusalem, so he took time to recuperate.

In his book, *The Freedom of Simplicity*, Richard Foster says,

> I function best when I alternate between periods of intense activity and of comparative solitude. When I understand this about myself I can order my life accordingly. After a certain amount of immersion in public life, I begin to burn out. And I have noticed that I burn out inwardly long before I do outwardly... I must learn to retreat, like Jesus, and experience the recreating power of God... Along our journey we need to discover numerous *tarrying places* where we can receive heavenly manna.[7]

In a crisis, all that needs to be done is multiplied and we must know our limits. We must understand our physical need of rest. We will only be able to accomplish what our physical bodies are capable of doing. Busyness can also cause us to disconnect from God. We must come to realize that rest is not *optional*. There is a verse in Ecclesiastes that speaks clearly about this—Ecclesiastes 10:10, "If the axe is dull and he does not sharpen its edge, then he must exert more strength."

Taking time for our physical needs is like sharpening our edge. So Nehemiah rested. Then, before he publicly laid out the plan, he reflected and reviewed the status of the work to be done. So after three days of rest, Nehemiah said, "I set out during the night with a few men. I had not told anyone what my God had put in my heart to do for Jerusalem" (2:12).

Honest Reflection

During this time, you begin to set the goals to carry out the plan. This is a time to assess the needs, research and gather the facts, and survey the situation. Notice too, that Nehemiah had a few men with him during these nighttime surveys. Nehemiah wanted input. He sought objectivity. In order for you to get to where you are going, you must know where you are! Honest reflection brings that about.

In order to lead this project, Nehemiah knew he needed a firsthand picture of what was to be accomplished. He personally scouted out the damage to the wall. Before Nehemiah began the job, he was determined to know everything—both the good and the bad details. This was not a time to be idealistic. This was not the time to be looking through *rose-colored glasses*.

I believe this is worth repeating: Too often our crisis causes us to panic which brings about only reactions. These knee-jerk reactions cause us to move out unprepared. Taking time to reflect brings about right responses—positive action based on confirmed levelheaded thinking. Nehemiah responded positively because he had a firm grip on reality. If you are living in a dream world, it will be much more difficult getting through your crisis. We must face facts honestly and be aware of the details.

Rallying Support

Once Nehemiah rested and after he reflected on the situation, he then rallied the support he needed. *Rallying* in a sporting event speaks of making a comeback! It's a recovery from a loss. It's about pulling through and crossing the finish line.

Think about it for a minute. Morale was probably at an all-time low for the people in Jerusalem. Their city wall was broken. Their homes were in need of repair. Discouragement and skepticism could have overruled. They could have said something like:

"Who is this guy?"
"Where did he come from?"
"Who does he think he is?"
"Rebuild this wall? We've already tried that."
"He's asking us to do the impossible!"

But they didn't. They responded to Nehemiah's call to rebuild by saying, "Let us start rebuilding. So they began this good work" (2:18).

What did Nehemiah say to get such a response? Here it is:

Then I said to them, "You see the trouble we are in: Jerusalem lies in ruins, and its gates have been burned with fire. Come, let us rebuild the wall of Jerusalem, and we will no longer be in disgrace." I

also told them about the gracious hand of my God
upon me and what the king had said to me.

Nehemiah 2:17–18

He asked the people to see what he saw. The problem was plainly and honestly defined. The solution was simply stated, and then he asked them to own the work, "Come, let us rebuild" (2:17). He reminded them that it was their wall, too. He made it clear that he didn't come to Jerusalem to rebuild its wall by himself. Nehemiah wanted them to know, if we're going to do this we've got to do it together. It is God's mission and idea, not mine. I'm his servant. And because it's God's idea, he will give us the victory. Psalm 127:1, "Unless the Lord builds the house, its builders labor in vain."

How does all of this fit in your situation? Do you need some rest? What action steps do you need to take based on what you know? Is it time to rally and make your comeback? It's an awesome thing when a plan comes together!

Before we move any further with our rebuilding story, there is an interesting dynamic to address. There's something else out there that is likely to come along during a crisis. Maybe you've experienced it already. It's *fear*. Where does fear come from? What will it do to us? Let's explore these questions in chapter four.

What's This About Fear?

For God did not give us a spirit of timidity, but a spirit of power, of love and of self-discipline.

2 Timothy 1:7

There is no fear in love. But perfect love drives out fear, because fear has to do with punishment. The one who fears is not made perfect in love.

1 John 4:18

You just survived a disaster, and it's beginning to look like there are good things just around the corner. The plan hasn't all come together, but you know that God has a plan and the things needed to get started are coming into place. But there's another matter that must be faced. It's personal; it's something that comes up from within each of us. It's *fear*.

Fear is something that will keep you from taking action. Fear is something that can prevent any further progress. We come to realize that there's a big task ahead of us, and we can be overwhelmed by it all. The thing that could have kept Nehemiah from moving out from where he was, was expressed as fear. He had never been where he was before, and he was afraid. He was standing at the threshold of a lot of things to tackle, and maybe his emotions were numb to some things, but he felt fear.

When Nehemiah's door of opportunity opened to share his heart with the king, he acknowledged that he was afraid, he said, "I was very much afraid, but I said to the king … the city where my fathers are buried [Jerusalem] lies in ruins" (2:2–3). He acknowledged fear and stated the problem. He didn't choke. He didn't let the paralyzing effects of fear stop him. He walked through the open door. Fear is something that comes along to destroy our faith in God's plan for us. Fear also comes along and causes us to doubt that a plan for moving out of our crisis is going to come together.

What are you afraid of today? In the bestselling book, *Who Moved My Cheese,* the authors ask a very penetrating question, "What would you do if you weren't afraid?" Fear often keeps us from taking the steps we know we need to take.[8]

What are some of the fears we can have when we're ready to launch out on a new venture? How about self-doubt, uncertainty, a lack of confidence, just to name a few fears. You'll have to discover what causes fear in

What's This About Fear?

you. But know this for sure: you'll have to overcome your fears before you can move forward.

Six days after Katrina, Pam and I found ourselves in line with thousands of other people to receive the basic essentials of life: water, ice, and MREs (meals ready to eat). It was at that moment that all that had happened in the preceding days became reality. *This really happened; it's not a dream. I'm standing in a distribution line with my wife.*

That day in particular, while in the distribution line, it hit me with a punch that seemed as hard as Katrina herself, and the waves of fear rippled through my mind. It wasn't the National Guard standing armed and at their posts—their presence was actually reassuring. It was an eerie feeling, almost like being in the middle of a dream, but it wasn't a dream. Previously, I had felt a numbness which kept me from accepting the situation, but on this day, it became a reality.

All of us in that line were in the same boat. No matter our status before the storm, we were all at the same place. The disaster had leveled the playing field. The sense of being self-sustaining or rolling up our sleeves and making it happen wasn't an option. We needed what was on those eighteen-wheelers, and this was the only place we were going to get it. This day was all about having our basic needs met. When Nehemiah pushed through fear, at his request, the king granted provisions. In the same way, provisions were being made for us and our fears were calmed.

Don't let fear have power over you. God knows the other side of where you are now, and he loves you! "… perfect love drives out fear" (1 John 4:18).

After Katrina, being in touch with reality was something we didn't do very well. We didn't say, "I choose denial." We were numb because of the shock we felt from our disaster. Who knows, maybe numbness had a purpose in lowering the level of our fear. As an example, let me share a story that happened to us. Pam's parents, George and Ginny Hall, live just a half a mile away from us. The day after Katrina, they drove to our house and asked if we wanted to go out with them to get some breakfast. The scope of Katrina and its devastation hadn't set in for them yet. There wasn't a restaurant open within two hundred miles of us. The thought of that was riveting for all of us! What are we going to do? What will happen to us? Will things ever be the same again? These questions and others caused fear to rise up and reality began to set in. We are in a *real* crisis!

The Difference Provision Makes

Remember the story I told you about our son, daughter, and two other friends coming down with a truck full of supplies? Well, when they returned home, they began to share with other congregations in central Illinois their experience on the Gulf Coast and the needs of the people.

Our son, Rod, continued to stay in touch with us regarding the needs of the people in our church. You might say that he was like an ambassador on behalf of these people who had experienced this unbelievable storm. God was working through Rod to provide some of the needs of our congregation.

After several conversations with Rod, the current needs of our congregation were being communicated to other churches in his area. Within a few weeks, a delegation from Northfield Community Church in Tremont, Illinois, led by Matt Miller and Gene Galat, came our way. They conveyed to us that they wanted to bring what the people of our congregation needed the most at that time. The unanimous answer from our congregation was meat! It was nearly a month, and everyone had lost all of their meat due to power outages, stores and restaurants weren't open yet, and believe me, those MREs were getting old. We were in desperate times, yet our fears were being overcome by these provisions. It was our sign from God that, though he was invisible, he was revealing himself in these visible ways.

It had been a long time since anyone had fixed a hamburger or made a roast dinner. When this group arrived from Illinois, they brought along with them basic essentials and over 2,000 pounds of meat for the folks of our church. The delivery of meat brought with it so much hope. After that, every time fear reared its ugly head, we could say with confidence, "We will make it" and "We will be able to do this; God will provide." It wasn't long, and our fears would be chased away.

At that time, this and other provisions meant survival for us and our community. For example, I can still see the mounds of clothing that were provided not only for our congregation, but for our church to distribute throughout our community. A group of young people led by Jenny Perizzolo and Jay Mills from the Denver and Aspen, Colorado area had gathered up supplies: cots, water, nonperishable food, baby items, and lots and lots of clothes. Volunteers from our church and a volunteer team that was here serving meticulously sorted through all of the clothing and essentials to create one of the first of many distribution centers at our church.

Another perfect example of our needs being met by others was the day that an eighteen-wheeler pulled onto our church parking lot with 40,000 pounds of supplies. Four churches from the Hartville, Ohio area had collected toiletries, baby items, nonperishable food, bath and bed linens, clothing, and paper supplies. There were so many supplies that volunteers from our church formed a *bucket brigade line* to hand off the items from the truck on the parking lot, up the stairs of our old sanctuary, and into the building. Once everything was inside, the contents of the truck literally filled the floor area of our old sanctuary.

As supplies continued to pour into our church, we established hours that we opened our church doors to distribute the food, clothing, and other supplies to the folks within our community. Volunteers and recipients were overwhelmed with the generosity of the people from the North. Honestly, at that time, I don't think that we or our benefactors realized how much these provisions gave us hope and helped to chase away our fears. Experiencing victory over our fears genuinely helped to solidify the plan for rebuilding our lives. As I look back, it is obvious that God in his infinite way was clarifying his plan and causing us to become more focused on the plan for the future.

On the fourth Sunday following Katrina, we gathered for worship. On this day, folks from Jubilee Mennonite Church in Meridian, Mississippi, came to our church with a special surprise. Duane and Elaine Maust brought a crew from their church along with Glen Welborn to fry catfish for everyone after the worship service. It was wonderful. They prepared a catfish dinner with all the fixings! Again, with this provision, God was confirming he had a plan and that he was going to take care of us.

Just as Nehemiah's fear was overcome by the building materials provided by the king, our congregation's fear was being overcome through these provisions of food. Believe it or not, 2,000 pounds of meat and a catfish dinner will go a long way to bring hope to a group of people that have just come through a hurricane. For us, each meal seemed to help dissipate our fears.

Challenges Keep Coming

And with that said, it didn't take long for us to be tested on this principle. Later, the same Sunday as the catfish fry, the church's leadership team and I had a meeting with our denomination's disaster agency—MDS. Two of their representatives, Willis Troyer and Karla Amstutz, were visiting us this day. We were looking ahead to the transition of our cleanup phase of relief into the much-needed rebuilding phase. In that meeting, we learned that we would not meet the agency's criteria to receive help with any rebuilding initiatives needed by either the church or for our people's homes. Although the agency had already received over two million dollars—and that was just the beginning of an incredible amount of money that was to come in to help the people whose homes were destroyed by Katrina—none of the families in our church would qualify to receive any of those funds. MDS seeks to help homeowners who do not have the financial resources to repair or rebuild their homes; however, most of the people in our congregation had home insurance or were in a higher income bracket, so they didn't meet the agency's criteria. When asked, "What we should do?" we were told that if there was going to be a rebuilding program for our church, we would need to do it ourselves.

This was unbelievable news; however, we remained in relationship with the agency, and they referred several volunteer teams to our rebuilding program. Their leaders were concerned, but their hands were tied at that time with existing policies.

Fears could have overtaken us that day. The leadership at the church felt surprised by the outcome of the meeting, but for some reason there was no fear. I realize now that the message of God's provision for our need had already been reinforced so powerfully that fear did not have a chance. God had a plan for us. On that day, we didn't know exactly how God would provide, but we knew everything would be okay because he would provide.

For us, God's plan was becoming clearer, and he was letting us know that he would provide! At this point, we were learning an important lesson of overcoming fear. In the next chapter, we'll share some principles that are significant for putting a plan into action. When you begin to get a handle on fear, you're ready for action.

How Do You Put Your Plan into Action?

But seek first his kingdom and his righteousness, and all these things will be given to you as well. Therefore do not worry about tomorrow, for tomorrow will worry about itself. Each day has enough trouble of its own. (Jesus)

Matthew 6:33–34

By this time, I was teaching from the third chapter of Nehemiah during our weekly Sunday morning gathering. As you remember, our Sunday worship service was the only regularly scheduled church activity we were experiencing throughout the week. Any other activity was not only impossible, it was a low priority compared to the insurmountable task that we faced. Relief and rebuilding, helping, and being helped were the minis-tries of the day.

We longed for *normal*, and we talked about it often; however, it would be a long time coming, not only for the church, but also for our jobs and individual lives. In the church's case, Sunday school and traditional annual events would eventually be reintroduced to our minis-try schedule. Hopefully, taking the right action steps would get us back to some sense of normal.

We were midway into Phase I of our relief efforts from the disaster—ten weeks of cleanup initiatives, when volunteers began to pour in. Daily, volunteers attended to the relief work—cutting up trees, putting blue tarps on roofs, and mucking out flooded homes. *Mucking out* was the process of tearing out and removing wet dry wall and anything else that got wet in a flooded home. Black mold was an enemy in those homes, and it spread rap-idly. Some of the members in our congregation had to tear out most, if not all of the drywall in their homes to totally eliminate the black mold problem, which basi-cally meant starting all over again.

The hot weather and difficult living conditions compounded the problems that we faced. Complet-ing the cleanup and moving forward was so important. With the living conditions as they were in the aftermath of Katrina, physical ailments for many were brought on by the stress, fatigue, and mold. My wife's parents went through the storm; however, the living conditions to follow were so unbearable that it was best for them to leave the area. One of our neighbors worked in Gulf-port, but he had rented a home in Pensacola, Florida, so his children could be in school. Traveling outside of the

Gulfport area was difficult at the time. We were grateful to have a way to get Pam's parents to the airport in Pensacola, so they could fly back to Illinois for the next four weeks. It was obvious that those who had known illnesses before Katrina worsened after the storm. To say these were difficult times does not fully describe it.

After ten weeks of cleanup, we began our rebuilding phase. We were looking forward to volunteer crews working on *permanent fixes*—like putting on shingles instead of blue tarps. Those blue tarps were everywhere. Miles and miles of blue tarps could be seen from any mode of transportation. After flights resumed into the Gulfport/Biloxi Airport, one of the first comments someone would make was how many blue tarps they could see from the airplane. As you drove along the Gulf Coast, you'd see them all day, and then at night, you would see them in your sleep.

As a result of that September meeting with MDS, we knew we would be involved in more than a short-term relief project. We needed to put more plans together so we could move forward into Phase II. We had already been hosting volunteer teams, and thankfully, they kept calling and coming. We had received some funds given directly to our church and fortunately, funds continued to come. In an effort to help both our contributors and us, First Mennonite Church in Morton, Illinois, and their pastor, Doane Brubaker, initiated and became the guardian of a Katrina fund for our church. This became a channel of God's supply of funding until our banks were opened again and we could establish our own Katrina fund.

Funds for rebuilding were available, and volunteer crews responded overwhelmingly to our needs. The leadership team of elders at the church made the decision that one hundred percent of the money given to our Katrina fund would be used for relief and rebuilding initiatives. We made our facilities available as a staging site for projects. Although our church building was in disrepair from the storm, we opened our facility as housing for the volunteer groups. The groups were thrilled because we had rooms for sleeping, bathrooms with showers, and a working kitchen. The volunteer teams that came were self-sustained: they took care of their own travel and expenses, brought their own food for a week and the people to do all the work in the kitchen. The only thing we had to offer outside of a building to stay in were projects for their volunteers to work on—lots and lots of projects.

Doesn't sound like much of an offer, does it? Well, maybe not from our perspective, but for the teams that came, they loved it. We were amazed how, week after week, teams of people would arrive at our church to work for a few days or for a week. At the end of an exhausting week of labor, we would gather around the teams to send them off and thank them for coming to the Gulf Coast to help us, and they would say, "No, we want to thank you. We came to help and bless you, but we are the ones who've been blessed." Many of those teams said they would probably return, and they did!

I think about how Brad and Teresa Houchin from Crosswinds Community Church in Bloomington, Illinois; Jeff and Angie Hegstrom and their church, Crosspoint Community Church in Eureka, Illinois; Jim Buckingham

How Do You Put Your Plan into Action?

from First Mennonite Church in Berne, Indiana; Carlisle Brethren Church in Carlisle, Pennsylvania led by Charles and Arlene Sieber; and Northfield Community Church led by Matt Miller and Gene and Joyce Galat from Tremont, Illinois, made several trips to south Mississippi and our church. All of these volunteer groups sacrificially gave large amounts of time to our congregation and its needs. These and all the other church groups volunteered their time, labor, and expertise to keep our disaster relief work on track. This was an incredible time in the history of our church. These volunteers left their fingerprints not only on the projects they completed but also on the lives of our church family.

Working Together as a Team

Here again the principles in Nehemiah helped us. In the third chapter, a number of times—twenty-eight to be exact—the phrase *next to them/him* or variations of it are found. The people in Nehemiah's day had a strategy to work as teams. People rallied to the challenge of "let us rebuild" (2:17). They worked together as a team. They partnered in the work to be done. They came alongside one another and worked together.

Nehemiah placed forty-four teams in forty-two places around the broken wall of the city of Jerusalem. The plan was moving forward, and it involved people working together. Working as a team affirms that we need each other. Of, and in our self, we're incomplete … we're less than whole.

When I think of teams, I'm reminded of the groups of youth that came from churches during the summer of 2006. Watching them serve made me feel good about the future! They came to our church serving self-lessly being led by awesome leaders like: Vern Hostetler (Hartville, OH) Andy Stuckey (Buhler, KS), Brad and Teresa Houchin (Bloomington, IL), Jonathan and Jane Bunn (Gulfport, MS), Jay and Sharon Burns (Gulfport, MS), Jeff and Angie Hegstrom (Eureka, IL), Wilmar Harder (Inman, KS), Rhonda Yoder (Goshen, IN), Jeff Dayton (Avon Lake, OH), Sam Coblentz (Hartville, OH), Darryl Lawler (Elyria, OH), Zach Brown (Springfield, MO), and Rob Job (Sedalia, MO). These groups of youth functioned in teams and accomplished so much while they were with us.

First Things First

Also, during our time of studying and teaching, two other strategies for action resonated from Nehemiah chapter three. One was the need for prioritizing. Where do we start? What's first, what's second, and what follows that? I'm sure it could go without saying, that there is a real need to prioritize when you are working with a major project like our relief efforts. Likewise, Nehemiah pointed out the necessity to prioritizing work efforts in facing the rebuilding of the wall.

Of all the gates in the wall around Jerusalem to choose, Nehemiah directed the work to begin at the Sheep Gate. Work not only began there (3:1), but it ended there as well (3:32). Throughout the chapter, there is a description of how Nehemiah placed teams in strategic positions and how they circled around the city beginning and ending at the Sheep Gate.

What was the Sheep Gate? A study of the gates in the wall is almost like a course in city planning. The gates allowed for various functions necessary for a city. The Sheep Gate had religious implications. Beyond this gate were the fields where shepherds tended their flocks. This gate was important because here is where the sheep—raised for sacrificial offerings—were brought into the city to the temple. The Sheep Gate was a gate of worship! During a time of worship at the temple, the sheep would be ushered in through this gate to be sacrificed on the altar. By making these sacrifices, the followers of God were continually acknowledging him and looking forward to the time that God's promised Son would come and give his life "once for all he offered himself" (Hebrews 7:27, 9:25–26, 10:9–10). "When he (John the Baptist) saw Jesus passing by, he said, 'Look, the Lamb of God!'" (John 1:36). It was through this same repaired gate that Jesus walked the week before going to the cross—"He himself bore our sins in his body on the tree, so that we might die to sins and live for righteousness; by his wounds you have been healed" (1 Peter 2:24).

Prioritizing in a crisis is not only knowing the sequential order of things but also keeping worship as a priority. In worship we express our love to God and stay connected to him. Ultimately, it is important to not only know *what's first*, but to know *who's first*.

Inside-Out

The other strategy, from this chapter, that helped us was the idea of working *inside–out*. This means beginning where you are and working outward. There is so much to do when you are in a crisis that a scattered, shotgun approach will not be effective.

To illustrate this principle, I would like to share a story with you that was written by Russell Conwell. It is a parable about finding what one is looking for, right where they are. Conwell was a minister and university founder and president in Philadelphia, in the early 1900s. *Acres of Diamonds* originated as a speech which Conwell delivered over 6,000 times around the world.[9]

The central idea of the story is that one need not look elsewhere for opportunity or achievement. The story is about a man that wanted to find diamonds so badly that he sold his property, left his family, and journeyed off in a futile search. When he returned to his hometown—old, tired, and poor—he discovered that the new owner of his house had found diamonds in the back yard of the property. If only he had applied the principle of *inside–out*, he could have been a rich man by never leaving his own back yard.

In the book of Nehemiah, we find that the teams of workers began where they were. They started working at their homes; they "made repairs opposite and beside their houses" (3:10, 23, 28–30). And then they worked their way out. They began their work where they were and worked *inside–out*. This concept can be illustrated by part of the preflight instructions given by a flight attendant before take-off of a commercial aircraft:

> If oxygen is needed in an emergency, an oxygen mask will be released from above you. Place the mask over your mouth and nose and tighten the strap. Pull down on the hose to start the oxygen flowing. Make sure you put on your mask, *first*, before assisting others—such as children.

The action plan for Nehemiah, for us, and for you in your crisis calls for creating teams, prioritizing, and beginning where you are. With this in mind, we must know that everything won't come easy. Things worthwhile are worth working for, and that work has its daily challenges.

Facing the Daily Challenges

After I looked things over, I stood up and said to the nobles, the officials and the rest of the people, "Don't be afraid of them. Remember the Lord, who is great and awesome, and fight for your brothers, your sons and your daughters, your wives and your homes."

Nehemiah 4:14

The daily challenges for Nehemiah came in the form of opposition to the work. In his case, there were actually people who did not want the project to succeed. Opposition and resistance came from those who did not want to see the wall of Jerusalem rebuilt. People were so opposed to the rebuilding of the wall that they began to express their resistance openly. It became so obvious that Nehemiah talked about a particular individual who "became angry and was greatly incensed" (4:1) when he heard of the rebuilding. This person used words to *ridicule* the work.

Keeping Focused

So what was Nehemiah to do? Instead of buckling under to these naysayers, Nehemiah said, "He and 'the people worked with all their heart'" (4:6). They made a conscientious decision to face their challenge. Together they determined to keep on with the work of rebuilding with their whole heart. This one decision not only helped them to overcome the negative atmosphere that they were in, it helped them to move forward with what the Lord had called them to do. Remember what Nehemiah said, "The people worked with all their heart" (4:6). They had become stronger because of the challenges. They were steadfast and resolved to see the job finished.

Know this one thing for sure… if you set out to accomplish something, there will be challenges. Your challenges may come from different directions and in different forms, but if you expect to be challenged and determined to stay focused, you won't be taken by surprise when it comes. You may already have what challenges you in mind. These challenges can lead to discouragement and stop you from working through your crisis. Even with their determination, the people in Nehemiah's day battled discouragement. In a later verse it says, "The strength of the laborers is giving out, and there is so much rubble that we cannot rebuild the wall" (4:10).

How do you respond to challenges? For some, this could be the end of the story. Others are determined to overcome and keep on. These are the ones who know in their heart that this is the thing that they need to be doing and they remain strong.

Let Faith Be the Response

Here's how Nehemiah responded to his challenge. First, from the beginning of the project, his focus was on what God could do by saying, "The God of heaven will give us success" (2:20). Sometime later in the New Testament, the Apostle Paul wrote, "If God be for us, who can be against us?" (Romans 8:31). "Who shall separate us from the love of Christ? Shall trouble or hardship or persecution or famine or nakedness or danger or sword?" (Romans 8:35). "No, in all these things we are more than conquerors through him who loved us" (Romans 8:37). Purpose, with God's help, to overcome your daily challenges!

Our mission was now transitioning from cleanup projects to rebuilding. It became apparent that we needed to do more for the families that we were working with. They needed permanent work done on their homes, and there were laborers to provide that need. Volunteer workers were saying things like, "Get us some shingles because we can put them on a roof almost as fast as *messin'* with blue tarps." And they were right. In the long run, it would be much better to go in and put on a shingle or metal roof, then the family receiving the roof did not have to worry about the next thunderstorm blowing off the blue tarp. So in December, four months following our disaster, we officially moved into Phase II, which was rebuilding homes.

The shift from cleanup to rebuilding was exciting, but it came with its challenges. As the work project cards continued to flood in, we knew we were in for a long journey. This job was bigger than all of us. This was truly a God assignment.

Where do you begin when the task is overwhelming? How will you be able to communicate the need to those that could possibly partner with you? And in our case, where was the money to purchase the materials for all of these rebuilding projects going to come from? Where are the skilled laborers, and how will they know about the rebuilding projects that we have? These were some of our daily challenges.

I'm sure by now, you are already ahead of me. You know what is about to happen, and you are right. God had the right people, at the right time, in the right place. Debbie Sullivan had strong administrative skills, so she scheduled crews and helped organize projects. There was also a group of men, willing and available leaders, from our church: Oren Miller, Tom Ward, Sam Estep, and Bill Ward who served as project leaders assessing the rebuilding projects and making lists of materials needed for each project.

The rebuilding work presented new challenges. Early on, a cleanup crew could come in and start cutting trees without much preparation on our part, but now if the crews were going to put up sheet rock or put on a roof, we needed to plan ahead. Projects needed to be assessed, necessary permits acquired, material lists had to be made, and then those materials—if they were available, needed to be purchased and delivered to the site before crews arrived. The project leaders had to

Facing the Daily Challenges

work weeks ahead. Volunteer teams that came in for a week would be ready to start out early on a Monday morning and continue from sunup to sundown throughout the week.

Multiply the above process by three or four because there were at least that many projects in process at one time. It was a juggling act to match the skills of the teams coming in with the type of rebuilding projects we might have scheduled for that week. If the crew was made up of roofers, dry walling projects were on hold that particular week. Our project leaders kept up with the status of each project providing coordination and continuity from week to week with each new crew arriving in south Mississippi; however, most projects were not completed in a week's time.

I don't mind saying, all of this was challenging. In working through your crisis, your challenge will be different, but you will be challenged during your rebuilding process. The mundane tasks in your life will seem bigger than they are. Things that need to be done will seem overwhelming. Things will look more complicated. You might even feel like it's impossible and want to give up. But here's where you've got to decide to move forward and "work with all your heart" (4:6) and keep your focus on God. He will "give you success" (2:20).

As the rebuilding phase went into full swing, the challenges and demands became greater and greater on all of us. I began to realize that I could not oversee the rebuilding efforts and meet the spiritual needs of our congregation at the same time. Although the volunteer crews were skilled and eager to serve and our home base of key administrative people and project leaders were in place, we were becoming weary. Just like Moses, we needed an Aaron and Hur to lift up our hands. We needed someone who could come in for several months and provide oversight to the rebuilding phase. We needed a project director—someone who could settle in for several months to provide continuity and oversight.

Being Open and Honest

So, just as we did when we needed funds or volunteer crews, we let our need be known. We were open and honest about what we thought God was doing, and we expressed our need. Does this resonate with you? Is there something left undone in your rebuilding process because you have not been totally open and honest yet? I believe one of the main deterrents God wants to break through in our lives during a time of rebuilding is pride. Pride says, "I don't need help; I can do it by myself." Pride also declares, "I don't want others to know what I really need." Pride is a personal challenge to overcome. If you need to do something about pride, let me encourage you to *go for it*, right now. Humble yourself, and ask for help. The scriptures tell us, "You do not have, because you do not ask God" (James 4:2).

So we began praying and asking for help. The job description for the project director read something like this:

> Skilled in contracting and home rebuilding.
> Excellent people skills. Willing to work long hours
> and able to do all this as a volunteer.

Facing the Daily Challenges

God heard our prayers for help, and he supplied our need. God chose to send us two incredible men who, along with their wives, more than fulfilled the expectations of our job description for that next year. Stan Roberts was the first to come. He and his wife, Joan, live in Gilbert, Arizona, and God put our church on their hearts to serve in the capacity of a project director. Stan said,

> As Joan and I watched the news of Katrina's devastation, we were compelled to find a way to aid. Our first visit of two weeks showed us a bit of how much more needed to be done. God gave us the courage to agree to go back for two months and help Gulfhaven members and others try to get back to *normal*.

And then, Jim and Lola Suderman, who live in Colorado Springs, Colorado, came to serve for the final six months of the rebuilding phase. Jim and Lola speak of what made their experience memorable:

- It was the feeling of being welcomed and included in the church family.
- It was the excellent processes that were in place for the church to heal from this experience.
- It was the absence of "victim complaints" by the members of the church in the aftermath of a traumatic and unforgettable disaster!
- It was the overwhelming willingness and generosity of the many volunteers that came to the Gulf Coast to help rebuild the area.

- It was the friendships that developed when participating in the repair and rebuilding work at the church.

- It was the way the Lord worked and blessed the lives of both volunteers and the members of the church.

Even now, as I am writing this, I can't put into words what I'm feeling about these two couples that have come to mean so much to all of us. They are truly examples of servant leadership at its best, and without a doubt their reward is eternal in the heavens!

From December of 2005 to December of 2006, we lived and experienced the scripture that says, "For nothing is impossible with God" (Luke 1:37). Things that seemed impossible became reality over and over again. One of our major challenges was matching jobs with the labor skills of volunteer crews: plumbers with plumbing jobs, roofers with roofing jobs, etc. It was both amazing and miraculous how the right people always were onsite at the right time. This was partly due to all the things done humanly by the gifted volunteers from our church, but we all knew that God was orchestrating the work! We were the instruments, and he was the conductor.

We were doing the day-to-day work, but all of the time there was a sense that God was behind the scenes. It was apparent that he wanted all of this to happen for us as much as we needed it. We merely put up the sails and he made the wind to blow! In your daily challenges, be encouraged to "work with all your heart" (4:6) and face all of your challenges.

At the end of November 2005, our son-in-law, Jeff Hegstrom our daughter, Angie, and their son, Blake, came with a crew for the second time from their church in Eureka, Illinois. During that week in November, their team helped us transition from over two hundred cleanup projects during Phase I to launching Phase II—the rebuilding phase. That was a groundbreaking week. Then, Brad Houchin, from Bloomington, Illinois, and his crew of skilled carpenters followed them and kept the ball rolling for the rebuilding phase.

I cannot close this chapter without giving special recognition to all of the crews that came to work along the Gulf Coast. First responders and crews that not only helped us with cleanup and rebuilding, but crews that poured their lives into our congregation. For us, they have a special place in our hearts. For them, some left a piece of their hearts on the Gulf Coast of Mississippi, and they continue to have wonderful relationships with us to this day.

Just like Nehemiah recorded the names of those that helped with the rebuilding of the wall later in Nehemiah chapter seven, we want to record the names as best we can, of the first responders and leaders of volunteer crews that are in our hall of fame.

John Beiler (Strasburg, PA), Nelson Horsemen (Cincinnati, OH), Troy Peachey and David Kniss (Arcadia, FL), Sam Fisher (Loysville, PA), Kurt Snyder (Arnold, MD), Amos Esh (Christiana, PA), Matt Miller (Tremont, IL), Kurt Pauls (Marshall, AR), Fritz Policelli (Arnold, MD), Brad and Teresa Houchin (Bloomington, IL), Scott Kauffman (Sarasota, FL), Ed Hammer (Lake Tomahawk, WI), Andy Johnson (Edgar, WI), Gene and Joyce Galat (Tremont, IL), Phil Eicher (Berne, IN), Steve Monahan (Etowah, NC),

Milford and Carolyn Lyndaker (Wardensville, WV), Jim Buckingham (Berne, IN), Dick Baner (Eureka, IL), Conrad Nagel (Berne, IN), Tom Rupp (Archbold, OH), Jeff and Angie Hegstrom (Eureka, IL), Eli Miller (Navarre, OH), Ted Williams (Bristol, IN), Carl Weaver (Elkhart, IN), Elam Steiner (Harrisonburg, VA), Ed Hauter (Mackinaw, IL), Archie and Jason Lohr (Ontario, Canada), Jonas Beiler (New Holland, PA), Phil Benner (East Earl, PA), Bruce and Marjorie Weber (Ontario, Canada), Stephen Miller (Heron, MT), John and Marvin Peachey (Allensville, PA), Brian Rufenacht (Archbold, OH), Ralph Blanch (Annville, PA), Robert Widemen (Ontario, Canada), Linford Musser (Lebanon, PA), Perry Miller (Hartville, OH), Eby Hershey (Gap, PA), Mike Richer (West Unity, OH), Ron Hostetter (Harleysville, PA), Stan Yoder (Angola, IN), Bernie Guyer (Willow Street, PA), Brent Keener (Lancaster, PA), Rocky Weaver (Blountstown, FL), Charles and Arlene Sieber (Carlisle, PA), Gary and Donna Koehn (Hesston, KS), Menno Kuhns (Trego, WI), Jerry Heaton (Bumpass, VA), Ken Wermuth (Glen Allen, VA), Enos Troyer (Russellville, KY), Jeffrey Long and Lois Hooley (Filer, ID), Glen Coblentz (Winesburg, OH), Ora Shetler (Kidron, OH), Conrad Beachey (Tremont, IL) Terry Zehr (Elkhart, IN), Mike Miller (Glide, OR), Sam Coblentz (Hartville, OH), Lewis Schmidt (Buhler, KS), Andy Stuckey (Buhler, KS), Wilmar Harder (Inman, KS) Merle Hostetler and Rhonda Yoder, (Goshen, IN), Vern Hostetler (Hartville, OH), Jeff Dayton (Avon Lake, OH), Mervin Miller (Applecreek, OH), Darryl Lawler (Elyria, OH), Amos Schwartz (Berne, IN), Zach Brown (Springfield, MO), Ron Job (Sedalia, MO),

Morris Nading (Hope, IN), Bob Philpot (Phoenix, AZ)

We thank God for all of these leaders who faithfully brought crews to the Gulf Coast. For over a period of fourteen months, a total of over 1,100 volunteers—from twenty-two states and Canada—came our way. Each and every one of them did their part in making what seemed impossible, possible.

Our rebuilding challenges were being overcome with help from those that came our way. In a way, they lifted us up and carried us through our crisis. Now, it was time for us as individuals to process our losses and begin to stand strong, again. We will see why this is an important next step in chapter seven.

Beginning to Stand Strong Again

> Get rid of all bitterness, rage and anger, brawling and slander, along with every form of malice. Be kind and compassionate to one another forgiving each other, just as in Christ God forgave you.
>
> Ephesians 4:31–32

Survival mode is an interesting phenomenon and people live in that mode in a multitude of ways. All too often, we can look back after a crisis and see that we acted out of character during that time. One of the true tests of our character is how we treat other people when we are under pressure; and we can learn some things about ourselves from this.

Learning from Our Reactions to Others

Why is it that *the survival of the fittest* is idealized—especially if it means climbing over someone else? It seems to me that the Golden Rule may be a better fit: "Do unto others as you would have others do unto you." Jesus spoke these words in his Sermon on the Mount: "Do not judge, or you too will be judged. For in the same way you judge others, you will be judged, and with the measure you use, it will be measured to you" (Matthew 7:1–2).

How much do we follow Christ's example of considering others? Sometimes, under pressure, we turn it around—doing unto others as they do unto us! In other places in the Bible we read, "Love your neighbor as yourself." This was Jesus' response when he was asked for the most important commandment. In Matthew 22:37, 39—He replied, "Love the Lord your God with all your heart and with all your soul and with all your mind." Then Jesus said, "And the second is like it: 'Love your neighbor as yourself.'" The Apostle Paul said,

> Do nothing out of selfish ambition or vain conceit, but in humility consider others better than yourselves. Each of you should look not only to your own interest, but also to the interests of others. Your attitude should be the same as that of Christ Jesus.
>
> Philippians 2:3–5

Consider a couple who is in the middle of a major crisis in their marriage. Both the husband and the wife will have a hard time focusing on the other person's needs because their own needs seem so much greater. Isn't it interesting though that when each person looks to the needs of the other—not regarding what they need—that their own needs end up being met, and the vicious cycle of isolation and self-centeredness is broken.

Something like this happened in the fifth chapter of Nehemiah. Some of the people were out for number one—themselves. They were in the mode of survival at any cost, even if that meant hurting someone. And the odd thing is it didn't matter how close they might be to someone else, they were going to climb over that person to get to where they wanted to go. Nehemiah exhibited true leadership in his response. He said, "When I heard their outcry and these charges, I was very angry. I pondered them in my mind ..." (5:6–7). Again, we see that Nehemiah was not a reactor, but a responder. After he identified the issue he "... called together a large meeting to deal with them" (5:7). Nehemiah put the issue on the table and the wrongdoers, "... kept quiet, because they could find nothing to say" (5:8). Nehemiah's final words were, "What you are doing is not right. Shouldn't you walk in the fear of our God ..." (5:9). The offenders final response was, "We will give it back. And we will not demand anything more from them. We will do as you say" (5:12).

When we have experienced loss, we feel hurt. And, when we're hurt, we act out in unusual ways. For some reason, we hurt back, and we act selfishly and demanding.

Why is it that we often hurt the ones we love? Why do we sometimes get irritated with those closest to us?

The work of rebuilding for the people in Nehemiah's day was taking its toll. All of this internal friction came on the heels of what we've already seen in chapter four. The people were becoming discouraged and tired. "The strength of the laborers is giving out, and there is so much rubble that we cannot rebuild the wall" (4:10). All this came at an interesting point in chapter four—when the work was half done. "…We rebuilt the wall till all of it reached half its height" (4:6). Fatigue had set in and what remained to be done was overshadowed by what they had already accomplished. They were discouraged, and their patience with each other had worn thin. So our response at the halfway point is critical in beginning to stand strong again.

It's Always Right to Do What Is Right

Nehemiah was a brave arbitrator, and a threat to the progress of the rebuilding was prevented. He models reconciliation for us. Nehemiah's concern for what was "right" (5:9) made the difference. When we are in the middle of our journey back during a crisis, doing what is right will help us stand again, and we can keep moving forward. Yes, we realize that we are not where we want to be, but we have come a long way, and we are not where we used to be. So, we need to keep on working and remember to keep on "doing what is right" (5:9).

In the New Testament book of Hebrews, the writer admonishes us to "Consider him (Jesus) who endured such opposition … so that you will not grow weary and lose heart" (Hebrews 12:4). Then the brother of Christ, James, begins his letter by saying,

Consider it pure joy, my brothers, whenever you face trials of many kinds, because you know that the testing of your faith develops perseverance. Perseverance must finish its work so that you may be mature and complete, not lacking anything.

James 1:2–4

Our objective is to stand strong again and to continue to move forward. Be aware that forward motion causes friction. Conflicts are going to happen when you are trying to make progress and especially when you are under pressure. People may not fully understand what you are going through or they may feel that you need to be approaching the matter in a different way. If this is the case, you will need to ask the Lord for wisdom as you seek out the best way to reconcile your differences.

The Goal - Reconciliation

Nehemiah models the reconciliation process in chapter five. Here is what happened: There were Jewish men who "raised a great outcry against their Jewish brothers" (5:1). It seems that in this case money was an issue and there were those who were taking advantage of the needs of others. The first step, Nehemiah took was to listen to both sides, "I pondered them in my mind" (5:7). Then he declared to the lenders, "You are exacting usury from your own countrymen!" (5:7). The next step, which can often be the hardest part in the reconciliation process, is getting both parties together and making things right. Reconciliation comes when the people involved in the situation: acknowledge their part, repent of wrong actions, seek forgiveness, and forgive the other person. The offenders in the incident Nehemiah recorded said, "We will give it back, and we will not demand anything more from them. We will do as you say" (5:12). When we respond to a conflict in the right way, we are able to stand strong.

Resiliency

Contrary to Nehemiah's day, as I think of the responses of resiliency of the people along the Mississippi Gulf Coast, I am still amazed how everyone pitched in and helped their neighbors up and down their street or road. Yes, there were shady contractors and there was price gouging; however, these situations were overshadowed with the many good things that were happening.

During the rebuilding time, the Coastal residents were living in their own damaged home, or they were living in a tent or trailer. As we transitioned to rebuilding, it was not uncommon to hear someone saying, "Help my neighbor. I'm *gonna* be okay," or, "There's so many other people worse off than me; start with them." Stop and think about this for a minute. The person who was able to stay in their home—even if it did have a blue tarp and storm damage—pointed us to the person living in a trailer. The person in the trailer, whose home was either water logged or leveled, pointed us to the person living in a tent. How humbling. What an example to all of us to consider the needs of others more than we consider our own needs, and yet, practically, we needed to start somewhere if we were going to get the rebuilding process moving.

In an attempt to bring some sense of order to our new phase of rebuilding, we needed to put some systems in place. We needed a strategy. Gratefully, with the help of MDS—Ted and Eleanor Shaddick and Lydia Weikel, conducted non-bias interviews with those that needed their homes rebuilt. They assessed the damage, created a prioritized list of projects, and discovered if the family had irrecoverable losses from the hurricane. Everyone yielded to their recommendations—all of the local people involved in the rebuilding phase, the volunteers who traveled in, and the recipients of the work.

A major benefit from the interviews was the ability to finally measure the magnitude of the loss created by Hurricane Katrina for the folks of our congregation. In the process, we discovered that some people did not have insurance because they lived in areas that had never flooded before, so flood insurance had not been required before Katrina. Some people did have insurance, but depending on their circumstances, the insurance may or may not have covered all of the damages incurred during the storm. As the projects came in, the need for more funding grew, so it was necessary for us to be back on our knees again.

Each new day brought its own challenges. More skilled crews were needed to accomplish the tasks that were set before us; and prayer, communication, and coordination became a lifeline for the numerous projects ahead of us.

As we followed the criteria set before us, we began to work one project after another, and we even expanded the circle of those who could be helped in the coming months. One of the early rebuilding projects was the home of Rose Fletcher, a member of our church. Rose worked at Stennis Space Center, where thankfully, she was able to be housed during and immediately after Katrina. Unfortunately, Rose's home did not fare as well as she did. Her home in Diamonhead—a small village west of the church—had taken in five feet of water. The water line on her walls was evidence that the water was sustained for a greater part of that day.

The homes where Rose lived in Diamondhead were not in a flood zone, but the magnitude of the storm had pushed the water up from not only the Gulf, but from every bayou and lake around that area. It was a double-edged sword for Rose—a flooded home with no flood insurance meant her damages would not be covered.

In an effort to better describe the situation, let me give you a word picture of the area. Diamondhead is actually north of Interstate 10 that runs parallel with the Gulf Coast and just above the bay between Pass Christian and Bay St. Louis to the south. Here is what's unbelievable—the water level at that exit on I-10 lapped over the overpass bridge. To this day, every time I drive under that overpass, I think about that event, and it brings with it a flashback of memories. And then, almost instantaneously, my mind goes to Rose's reconstructed home. What a wonderful story of restoration and resiliency after the storm.

Like Rose, others evacuated before Hurricane Katrina made landfall. One of those evacuees was Robert Mixon. Robert, a recent widower, sent me an E-mail the Sunday morning before Katrina, saying, "I am evacuating, and this storm looks like it's going to be a *killer*." Little did he know at that time that his prediction would be so accurate.

Robert lives in Biloxi about a mile north of the beach. Following Katrina, it was several weeks before the residents could return to their homes because the area was so dangerous. Where there was once homes, lots were covered with debris, and the infrastructures had been compromised. I will never forget the day that we could finally get into that area. Pam and I drove over to see if Robert was at home. For blocks, homes had been leveled by the storm surge, and then, out of all of the rubble, stood Robert's home. Robert was one of the fortunate ones in that area—he still had a home that was standing.

Unfortunately, the mold in his home was spreading rapidly from being closed up in the hot and humid conditions following the storm, and Robert's watermark was at eight feet. The one hundred-mile-an-hour winds had ripped away at the structure, and the waters to follow brought their destructive forces.

When the volunteers came to Robert's house during the cleanup phase, they had to *muck out* the inside of the house. Only this *mucking out* job required an extra step—stripping everything from the outside of the structure, as well. When the volunteers were finished, they turned around to see this huge pile of rubble in the front of his home. The pile of rubble was so large that it was like a mountain casting a shadow on this bare, studded frame of a house.

Everything inside the house was destroyed by Katrina. The contents of the house were a total loss, and everything had to go. One of the saddest memories I can recall was watching Robert as he painstakingly purged through his belongings. Standing next to the pile of rubble outside of the structure of his home, Robert began to go through box after box of personal belongings. One box was filled with show ribbons that Robert had won from championship horse shows. When we inquired about the ribbons, Robert began to reminisce about the days when he showed prized horses. Controlling his emotions, Robert began to throw the water-damaged ribbons on the pile of rubble. Quietly, I asked, "Don't you want to try to save one of the ribbons as a memory?"

With tears in his eyes, Robert said, "No, those ribbons are *just stuff.*"

It's just stuff. We heard that a lot as people began to rebuild their homes. What a valuable lesson for all of us to learn. The folks on the Gulf Coast came to realize that all though the things in life are nice and they may make our lives a little easier, they are truly *just stuff.* The most important things in life are the relationships that we build. There is no value you can put on personal relationships, and they are truly irreplaceable.

In the spring of 2006, Robert's home was completely rebuilt, and it was time for him to move back into his house. Conscientiously, Robert purchased every item that went back into his home with money he had been blessed with. What a thrill to witness his joy in all the provisions being returned to him after the storm.

There is story after story of people in need and people being blessed by the generosity of donors and volunteer workers. Volunteer workers left their jobs in the north, took their vacation time, paid their own expenses for travel, and purchased and cooked their own meals. Workers, during that time, put in long days and slept at night on air mattresses on our church floor. These workers helped us when we couldn't stand on our

Beginning to Stand Strong Again

own so that one day we could get to a place of standing strong again.

Standing Strong and Being a Servant Leader

These volunteers taught us so much about servant leadership. We hear that term and we read about it, but I'm grateful to have been a witness of seeing servant leadership in action. At the end of chapter five, Nehemiah shows us the kind of stuff he was made of. After he helped reconcile the two groups, he was promoted to governor. In verses fourteen through nineteen of chapter five, we see that Nehemiah was a servant leader.

Let's take a glimpse of Nehemiah, the servant leader. Nehemiah said, "But the earlier governors—those preceding me—placed a heavy burden on the people …" (5:15). He never "lorded it over the people" (5:15). "Instead, I devoted myself to the work on this wall," he says (5:16). Also in this verse we learn that "we did not acquire any land" (5:16). He served with no regard for money. And then, we see that he was willing to serve others. He provided for the needs of over a hundred and fifty workers out of his own pocket. That great number of people "ate at my table … Each day one ox, six choice sheep and some poultry were prepared" (5:17–18). And we find out that Nehemiah, " … never demanded the food allotted to the governor, because the demands were heavy on these people" (5:18).

A servant leader! It's interesting that the same three marks found in Nehemiah—not lording over the people, not greedy for money, and a willingness to serve others—are also found in 1 Peter 5:2–3. Actually, Peter lists them in reverse order. "Be shepherds of God's flock that is under your care, serving as overseers—not because you must, but because you are willing, as God wants you to be; not greedy for money, but eager to serve; not lording it over those entrusted to you, but being examples to the flock" (1 Peter 5:2–3).

So many other rebuilding stories could be told about servant leaders—the volunteers that made all of the following rebuilding projects possible. John and Carolyn Begue had twenty-seven feet of storm surge come through their stilted home in Pass Christian. I remember the hardwood floors of Trudi Mullins' home in Gulfport swollen from the three feet of water it sustained. The floors looked like the rolling waves on the ocean. Marc and Myrna Luckey lived twenty-three homes from the beach in Long Beach before Katrina. However, after the storm, the Luckey's home was the third home standing from the beach because so many homes in their block had been leveled by the storm. When the roads were cleared and you could walk through their neighborhood again, the debris was eight feet high across the entire block. Thankfully, because of the efforts of servant leaders, all of these families are back in their homes.

During the yearlong rebuilding phase, our church was involved in over eighty rebuilding projects. As a result of people helping people, each person that was helped began a journey to stand strong again. It was for sure that things weren't as they used to be. Things weren't normal; however, people were learning to accept a new kind of normal.

Remember that I mentioned earlier that our church building needed to be rebuilt, too? Although volunteers filled our Sunday school classrooms and sanctuary with cots and air mattresses to sleep on, and they cooked their meals in our storm-damaged kitchen throughout the week; we as a congregation continued to meet on Sundays. Our damage was significant from the storm; however, besides the new roof that was put on immediately after the storm, it would not be until March of 2006 that we would be able to address any of our church's building needs.

In the next chapter, I want to address the topic of being a finisher. Often, it is easier to start a project than it is to see that project to completion.

How Do You
Keep On Track
and Finish?

So the wall was completed on the twenty-fifth of Elul, in fifty-two days. When all our enemies heard about this, all the surrounding nations were afraid and lost their self-confidence, because they realized that this work had been done with the help of our God.

Nehemiah 6:15–16

Starting something is one thing. Finishing is another! Finishing is especially important when it comes to working through your crisis.

You may be saying, "I know of some unfinished things that are actually popular." For example, if you are a connoisseur of art, you may know of an unfinished piece of art that you like or perhaps you enjoy the drama and intrigue of an unfinished symphony. Both of these examples may be exceptions to the rule, but normally finishing a project is essential.

Look at the Apostle Paul; he is a pretty good example for us. Paul writes in his last letter what some have called his *last will and testament*. In the last chapter of 2 Timothy, Paul wrote,

> I have fought the good fight, I have finished the race, I have kept the faith. Now there is in store for me the crown of righteousness, which the Lord, the righteous Judge, will award to me on that day—and not only to me, but also to all who have longed for his appearing.
>
> 2 Timothy 4:7–8

I would gather from what Paul had to say that being a finisher is a good thing!

I know it may be tempting, but don't take any shortcuts in your rebuilding process. Jesus himself was tempted to shortcut his appointed three years of ministry when he was enticed by Satan in the wilderness. But praise God, he overcame and finished. Remember his words on the cross? He made a powerful declaration saying, "It is finished!" (John 19:30).

Don't Be Enticed By Something That Looks Better or Seems Easier

When we read Nehemiah's story in the sixth chapter, we learn that he and the people finished their rebuilding project. "So the wall was completed ... When all our enemies heard about this ... they realized that this work had been done with the help of our God" (6:15). They finished, but it didn't come without the temptation of ending early or taking a shortcut.

When the project is overwhelming and we start to get tired, it's easy to convince ourselves that the job is done. We may begin to justify what we have done by saying, "This is good enough." Beware that you may find yourself being tempted to say, "Even though I'm not completely finished, things sure seem better than when I began all this work."

What were distractions that tempted Nehemiah? Early on in chapter six, the enemies of Nehemiah began to come together to negotiate another plan. All of a sudden, people who were enemies were trying to become friends. They were saying, "Come, let us meet together in one of the villages" (6:2). Something seemed a little fishy to Nehemiah. Interestingly, as we continue reading the storyline, we discover that the enemy came knocking on Nehemiah's door "four times" (6:4) with the same friendly invitation, but Nehemiah didn't give in to the lure of something different or an offer for something that seemed better than what he was doing. Instead, Nehemiah realized the importance of finishing the job. He looked forward to the gratification and reward of knowing he and the other workers had finished the wall. Beware of the lure of something else before you finish what you are doing.

This became a personal matter for me during our time of relief and rebuilding. In all honesty, there were often days that I felt discouraged and depressed. Ministry—the way I had known it for the past thirty-five years—was now so different. Hopes and dreams of what the ministry at the church might be seemed to be shattered. In the darkest of days, it was tempting to think, *This isn't why I came to Mississippi; there must be something else that the Lord wants me to do.*

When discouragement was just about to take over, there were two sustaining factors that kept me going. One was realizing that even though I didn't know about Hurricane Katrina when Pam and I moved to south Mississippi, God did. This line of thinking—that God knew about Katrina and must have a purpose in it— kept me going. The other was a conversation that I had with a man I had never met until after the storm.

In January of 2006, I met Walter Sawatsky. In God's providence, he brought Walter my way to deliver a message I needed to hear. You see, Walter was a pastor in south Florida when Hurricane Andrew struck. In a conversation with Walter, he told me that shortly after Andrew's devastation that he was informed that "more than likely two-thirds of all of the pastors and ministers in his area would no longer be in that area two years later." He said, "They told me that based on previous statistics we would either be out of the ministry or moving somewhere else to serve." At the time, that statistic surprised me, but I was also relieved to know that the feelings of quitting or moving were common. From that time on, that conversation with Walter came to my mind quite often. That particular information helped me to process discouraging thoughts and feelings; and to consider God's sovereignty in my journey through this difficult time. "Many are the plans in a man's heart, but it is the Lord's purpose that prevails" (Proverbs 19:21).

How Do You Keep On Track and Finish?

Think about it, Nehemiah continued to stay focused on finishing the wall. For him, the best way to keep from being *distracted* was by staying *attracted* to God's vision and plans. Paul says in the New Testament book of Philippians, " ... being confident of this, that he who began a good work in you will carry it on to completion until the day of Christ Jesus" (Philippians 1:6).

The Blessing of Staying Focused and Finishing

The rebuilding projects at our church were moving forward during the first months of 2006. People were being encouraged as their homes were being rebuilt, and Stan Roberts was handing the baton as project director over to Jim Suderman. It seemed as though we were getting a second wind of sorts, but we were still far from the finish line.

There was also another project that was on the back burner—rebuilding the church. Early on, a new roof had been put on—two hundred squares in all. The storm had also destroyed the church's steeple, and our goal to replace it before Thanksgiving of 2005 was met. The replacement of the church's steeple was a symbol so meaningful to us at the time; it meant that we will rebuild. We had a new roof and steeple, but there was so much more that needed to be done, and the church building was far from being finished.

During Katrina, the shingles on the church roof peeled back, and the sheeting tore off completely in places, exposing the church building to a lot of water. Ceilings and walls in several areas of the building had gotten wet, and the pine ceiling and the insulation in our sanctuary had been soaked and destroyed.

Fortunately, the main structure of the building had not been compromised, so we were able to use the building for Sunday services and to host volunteer teams. Some of the first steps were to remove all of the drywall from areas of the building that had gotten wet, as well as the warped pine ceiling and wet insulation from the main sanctuary.

A specific and important story comes to mind when I think about the removal of the pine ceiling in our church's sanctuary. In the mid-90s, when the new addition had been built on to the existing structure, the church had decided to hang yellow pine for the sanctuary ceiling. A former leader in our church, Solan Johnson, had played a significant part in the placement of that pine ceiling. On the last night of construction, Solan—along with the other men hanging the pine, decided to write their names on the final board before nailing the board in place.

Now, that beautiful yellow pine ceiling that those men so painstakingly hung had to be torn down to remove all of the warped boards and soaked insulation. I can still remember standing in the middle of all of the dust from the demolition of the ceiling when Marie Johnson walked into the church sanctuary. While the demolition crew we hired was tearing down the pine ceiling, Marie proceeded to tell me the story that I just told you. At that time, I knew that this was very meaningful to her because her husband had since passed away. After Marie left, I remember saying to the demolition crew, "If you find a board with the name Solan on the back of it, could you bring it to me?"

Within the next couple of days, one of the workers came with a big smile, saying, "I found the board." How exciting to know that out of all of that destruction something so precious had been found. What a great symbol for all of us to hang on to—a symbol of a new beginning for our church out of something that represented a lot of hard work and memories of good things that had passed.

Although we were beginning to see some progress, the tasks that were ahead of us seemed insurmountable. Not only did we need to work on the interior of the building, the exterior siding had to be replaced due to the damage from the hundred-mile-per-hour winds of Katrina.

Together, the leadership decided to begin rebuilding the church in March of 2006. At the same time, we would continue rebuilding homes at the pace that it was already going. Although, this would mean double the work and activity taking place, the leadership of the church felt we needed to get started.

Although we are in a warmer climate, our heating bills during the winter months literally went through the ceiling in 2005 with heat pumps running twenty-four/seven. And cooling the building during warmer weather meant that air conditioners were running all of the time because we had no insulation in the walls and ceilings that had to be replaced in the building. With this in mind, our goal was to get the church building finished before the winter of 2006.

Now, we needed another project director—one to replicate a similar rebuilding program to what was happening in the home rebuilding phase. One person immediately came to the minds of the leadership—Ed Miller. Ed and his wife, Ethel, visited us on the Gulf Coast shortly after the landfall of Hurricane Katrina. Ed recounts that visit by saying,

> To most everyone, there comes an epical moment that lingers as a monumental landmark in the life of that person. Hurricane Katrina provided one of those lasting impacts in my life. When Pastor Nelson Roth gave me the first guided tour, my mind could hardly wrap itself around what my eyes were seeing. Block after block, mile after mile of rubble; cement steps leading to nowhere. Gulf Coast Antebellum homes that had withstood previous hurricanes now were forever gone. Homes, businesses, motels, casinos, churches had disappeared or remained only as gutted skeletons that had to be demolished in the cleanup phase that would precede any rebuilding.

Knowing the impact that Katrina had made on him, we knew that if there was anyone who could lead such a project, it would be Ed. But would he be interested in helping now? Would he be available to come for four months or longer? And could he start in March?

He was the lead contractor when the new church sanctuary was built in the mid-90s. It was a long shot, but we made the call. Ed, a retired minister, is known and loved by all the folks at our church. Ed was a former pastor at Gulfhaven—he knew the area, he knew the people, he knew all about the building structure.

Oh, I forgot to mention one more factor—Ed, at that time, was eighty-four years young.

When we made the call, Ed nearly jumped through the phone at the opportunity. Then we asked Ethel, his wife, and him to pray about a four-month commitment. Also, we knew that they would want to consult with their family that lived in the Aurora, Colorado, area near them before making their decision. Two days later, Ed called and said, "I'm on my way."

Well, with a project director in place for the church, we needed to secure volunteer work crews. So, we put out the word about the church rebuilding project. Many crews and individuals played such an important part, but the first two crews that came in and worked under the direction of Ed were a model for all that were to follow.

Ron Hostetter from Salford Mennonite Church in Harleysville, Pennsylvania, was already scheduled to bring in a crew the first of March. There were twenty-five skilled carpenters in that group, and they brought an eighteen-wheeler loaded with tools and scaffolding. Amazingly, this crew arrived shortly after Ed was on the scene in Mississippi.

Ed knew the building so well that he had prepared material lists even before he left Colorado. This was essential so that Ron and his crew would have work to do and materials to work with when they arrived. Their primary job the week they were in Gulfport was to tear off the old siding of the church building, make exterior repairs, and reside the entire church building with Hardi plank. Watching them work was a sight to behold. They had a system, and they worked as a team. Each person knew what his job was, and they eagerly worked and completed their tasks. Their goal was to be finished in a week, and they met their goal. Ron said, "We don't want to leave until the project is finished." And finish they did. The crew literally put on final trim boards just minutes before their departure.

While that work was going on, Ed was getting things ready for the crew coming in the next week. They would, among other things, be replacing 7,000 linier feet of Southern yellow pine ceiling boards for the sanctuary. The ceiling in our church sanctuary rises to a twenty-four foot peak in the center. Everyone knew that this would be a major challenge to complete in a week, but this was the goal the crew leader, Charles Sieber, and Ed had set in advance.

Because building materials were scarce, Ed began to research lumber companies outside of the Gulfport area that carried the Southern yellow pine for the ceiling. We thought the problem was solved when we discovered a mill located in Alabama; however, as the time neared for the team from Carlisle, Pennsylvania, to come, we still did not have the yellow pine. Just at one of the most critical times in the church rebuilding process, Ed decided to check out a local lumberyard. Amazingly, the person that ended up helping Ed had worked for another contractor's supply firm when the church originally built the new sanctuary addition ten years prior. Fortunately, this person was able to locate the 7,000 linear feet of pine that we needed, and it was delivered just in time.

In an effort to be ready for the carpenters that were coming with Charles Sieber and his wife, Arlene, the pine boards arrived at the church two weeks prior and were being sanded and varnished by volunteers that were staying at the church. The folks coming with Charles from Carlisle Brethren in Christ Church in Carlisle, Pennsylvania, numbered sixty volunteers. They had incredible skills among them, and they operated like a well-oiled machine. Along with the sanctuary ceiling, they poured the foundation, framed the floors, and built the roof trusses for a new kitchen expansion; plus they finished the roof decking over the new addition. Like the volunteer group before them, they finished all they came to do. They were an awesome group to watch—from the food preparation crew in the kitchen that prepared three meals a day to the folks who did laundry every day for the workers. They were all finishers.

The new kitchen expansion was an example of the good things that come out of something bad. The storm did damage to the church's old kitchen, tearing the outside door off its hinges and allowing a lot of water to come in. Also, the kitchen was small, particularly with the size of groups we were hosting. So, the folks from Carlisle said, "We'll build a kitchen addition when we are there in March." The kitchen and another room were designed beyond the existing outside wall, which would mean that the seating area in our fellowship hall would also be enlarged. The church leaders announced a fundraising campaign to determine the feasibility of this project. We did not want to use any of our insurance money or the church's relief fund money for this project. God's hand in the building addition was evident when, within three weeks of this being presented—the first part of February—the cost of the project was either raised or promised to be given by Easter Sunday!

Nehemiah summed it up this way with his people,

> So the wall was completed on the twenty-fifth
> of Elul, in fifty-two days. When all our enemies
> heard about this, all the surrounding nations were
> afraid and lost their self-confidence, because they
> realized that this work had been done with the
> help of our God.
>
> Nehemiah 6:15

Because of the insurance settlement for church damages,
there were several options for getting the work completed. We could hire subcontractors and receive bids for
the various projects; however, interestingly, no contractors were available. These were unusual times along the
Coast with so much work to do. The other option was
to schedule volunteer crews who were willing to work on
the church, knowing that the insurance money saved on
the labor would be used to rebuild homes through the
church's Katrina fund. In talking with Ed at the time, I
remember him saying that the second alternative must
have been God's plan. There was a surge of some of
the finest professional carpenters, framers, electricians,
plumbers, dry-wallers, finishers, and painters pouring in
from far and wide.

There were so many wonderful people who helped
us finish the work on our church building. I wish there
was enough time and space to write a paragraph about
each group who helped with the church rebuilding. I
do, however, want to mention Ken Wermuth and Jerry
Heaton, two men from Virginia, who stayed on the
church project for six weeks. Both of these men are
great carpenters. They not only completed some major

projects, they also went over the entire building inside and out, meticulously adding finishing touches. They are the type of laborers that not only work hard and long hours, but they are also the type that look for what needs to be done and do it without hesitation.

Finally, when we think about the work done on our church building, Steppin-Out Missions comes to mind pretty fast. John and Shirley Corley and Joel and Megan Corley lived in our church building for nearly two months during the summer of 2006. Along with the Corleys, members of their long-term leadership team were Jared Stutzman, Brandon Judy, Tyler Hudson, Carole Armentrout, Dave Spangler, and Tom Bishop.

During that time, these folks from Steppin-Out Missions and volunteer teams that joined them worked tirelessly on the church building. The Corleys also led crews that came to our church to work on a number of home rebuilding projects during our outreach phase.

In an E-mail that John and Shirley sent to me, they reflect on the obedience of God's people to respond and complete projects along the Gulf Coast.

> Never have we seen a spiritual knife do surgery on people's lives like we witnessed after Hurricane Katrina. God chose to level the playing field of need for everyone. For us, here at Steppin-Out Missions, one of the most obvious confirmations that we were to respond to the need was the obedience of people across our country contacting us asking what we were planning and how could they join us? People across our great states remembered how to respond and serve others. God's people were aware that he

could orchestrate this response and it was their opportunity to do Kingdom work!

Steppin-Out Missions is an awesome ministry based in Sugar Creek, Ohio. They provide a mission experience to church teams on foreign soil. However, following Katrina, John Corley was led to consider something different and that was to lead mission teams here in the states—to the Gulf Coast. We are grateful for our relationship with Steppin-Out Missions. Every time we walk through the church building, we recall those hard but glorious days that they spent with us. The Corleys will have a special place in the hearts of our congregation, forever.

When the Corleys left in the fall of 2006, Howard Walkinshaw, one of our church elders led in the completion of the remaining church rebuilding projects. Thanks to Howard and everyone in leadership that preceded him, we can look at our church building today and truly say that it is finished—nothing major was left undone. Like Nehemiah, we can say that "this work has been done with the help of our God!" (6:16).

What do we do next? What do you do once you reach your goal? So far, it's been all work. Could it really be the time to have a party? Remember the motto, "All work and no play"? If you are saying, "Now is the time to celebrate," you're right. In the next chapter, I will share with you our rebuilding completion celebration. It is time to talk about the importance of celebrating and intentionally having fun.

What's so Important about a Time to Celebrate?

Nehemiah said, "Go and enjoy choice food and sweet drinks, and send some to those who have nothing prepared. This day is sacred to our Lord. Do not grieve, for the joy of the Lord is your strength." Then all the people went away to eat and drink, to send portions of food and to celebrate with great joy... From the days of Joshua... the Israelites had not celebrated it like this. And their joy was very great.

Nehemiah 8:10, 12, 17

By the end of 2006, we had finished the repairs on our church and we were in and continuing an outreach rebuilding ministry—Phase III. Wonderful volunteers from Buhler Mennonite Church in Buhler, Kansas, launched the outreach phase in April of 2006. They brought two teams on two successive weeks to begin this initiative. For the most part, homes of our church members were now completed, and we were beginning to reach out to others who needed help with rebuilding their homes. Although there was plenty of work to do, we felt that so much had been accomplished that we needed to stop and celebrate.

We started planning a celebration that would take place in January 2007. Events during the three-day celebration would include a church rededication, a home blessing for rebuilt homes, and a mortgage burning. Yes, you heard me right, a mortgage burning.

Rebuilding After a Disaster
Leads to Renewal and Renewal
is Cause for Celebration

Prior to Katrina, our church was anticipating a mortgage-burning service in September of 2005. God had been working in many wonderful ways at our church spiritually; one of the evidences of that was incredible monetary giving. Because the congregation was giving so faithfully, we were able to pay off the church's mortgage years in advance of the scheduled final payment. Unfortunately, the mortgage-burning celebration set for September 2005 was canceled and put on the back burner due to Katrina and all that followed. So, January 2007 became the new appointed time for our celebration of a number of things.

Our plans for the celebration weekend included gathering at the church to eat, sing, and hear great preaching on Friday night. Following an evening meal on Saturday, a time of dedication for homes that had been rebuilt were part of the special services. As a grand finale of the events on Saturday, a firework display lit up the sky. During the Sunday morning worship service, we experienced the mortgage burning followed by a meal and a time of fellowship resembling a family reunion. We were not just making plans to celebrate, we *needed* to celebrate, and just thinking about the weekend energized us.

One thing I don't want to forget to tell you about is what became known as Bunn's burger dance. It happened late on Saturday night, during the weekend of events scheduled for the celebration. Keep reading ... I'll tell you more about it later.

Likewise, in the book of Nehemiah, Nehemiah led the way for a celebration following the completion of the wall. In chapters seven and eight, he tells us that "After the wall had been rebuilt and I had set the doors in place, the gatekeepers and the singers and the Levites were appointed" (7:1). They were getting ready for a celebration. There was still work to do; verse four tells us that there were houses that "had not yet been rebuilt" (7:4). But there comes a time during the rebuilding phase in a crisis when you need to stop and celebrate. In the eighth chapter, we learn that "the people assembled as one man in the square" (8:1). Then Ezra came on the scene. He appears for the first time in the book of Nehemiah. He's the priest, the spiritual leader that led the people into a time of celebration with singing, worshiping, and listening to the Word. Ezra had been around, but he had not been mentioned up to this point. There was so much going on that the work of rebuilding actually overshadowed their worship. But now, the people were eager to worship. In fact, this large assembly requested Ezra to "bring out the Book of the Law" (8:1). Then, "He read it aloud from daybreak till noon ... and the people listened attentively to the Book of the Law" (8:3).

As a result of hearing the Word again, the people in Nehemiah's day cried, and streams of tears flowed down their faces. Their tears were tears of renewal. The people were reconnecting with God again in an intimate way. The tears were no doubt expressions of joy. The tears were also expressions of sorrow because of areas in their lives that did not line up with what they were hearing from the Word. Their conviction brought change, and the end result was joy.

The people in Nehemiah's day were under conviction because something was missing in their lives. In their case, it was to observe a certain feast and "to live in booths during the feast of the seventh month" (8:14). When they learned what was missing, they responded in obedience, and joy was restored in their lives. "From the days of Joshua son of Nun until that day, the Israelites had not celebrated it like this. And their joy was very great" (8:17). Is there something missing in your life? Has the work of rebuilding diverted your attention away from spiritual things? If you are ready for renewal, God is ready to bring joy into your life. Now, that's reason for a celebration!

Nehemiah and all of Israel were full of joy and quite possibly overwhelmed with all that the Lord had done for them out of their crisis and in the rebuilding of the wall. Their tears were tears of joy and gratitude. At one point in their celebration, Nehemiah knew just what the people needed. He said, possibly with a big grin on his face, it's time to eat, "Go and enjoy choice food and sweet drinks…This day is sacred to our Lord. Do not grieve, for the joy of the Lord is your strength" (8:10). And with those instructions, the entire crowd did just that—they "went away to eat and drink…to celebrate with great joy, because they now understood the words that had been made known to them" (8:12). There was a realization that the goodness of God was bringing renewal into their lives. Here's something you can take away with you from this section of the book—rebuilding after a disaster leads to renewal and renewal is cause for celebration.

During one of our planning sessions for our celebration at the church, we decided to use the phrase, "To God be the glory!" We truly felt that statement summed up what was in our hearts. The closer we got to the celebration, we could sense the anticipation and joy that it was bringing to our congregation.

For our celebration, we invited volunteer teams that had helped over the past fourteen months, first responders, as well as friends and family members of our church congregation to join us. One sweet lady who lives in Kansas now, but was a member of our church, Elsie Miller, said she was looking forward to the celebration more than she was looking forward to Christmas that year.

With every confirmation of people coming from a long distance, you could sense the excitement that the people in our congregation were feeling. All of us were so grateful for everything that these faithful servants of God had done for us during a time of great need. Ed and Ethel Miller, Jim and Lola Suderman, David and Esther Kniss, Stan Roberts, John and Joel Corley, Ken Wermuth and Jerry Heaton, our son Rod and his two boys, Chandler and Parker, and so many more traveled long distances to join us for those days of celebration. Not only was this the best celebration, it was a great reunion of so many people we love.

Gathering to Hear the Word

A key part of our celebration gatherings was a time of hearing the Word of God. On Friday night Karl Bernhard, from Amor Viviente in New Orleans, preached. On Saturday night, two former pastors, David Kniss and Ed Miller, delivered the Word. Then on Sunday morning, I brought a message from 1 Thessalonians about how the church in Thessalonica was a model church. Just like the people in Nehemiah's day gathered to hear the Word of God, we centered our thoughts around the Word during our celebration. The people in Nehemiah's day requested that Ezra "bring out the Book of the Law of Moses" (8:1). At the appointed time,

> Ezra opened the book. All the people could see him because he was standing above them; and as he opened it, the people all stood up. Ezra praised the Lord, the great God; and all the people lifted their hands and responded, "Amen! Amen!" Then they bowed down and worshiped the Lord with their faces to the ground.
>
> Nehemiah 8:5–6

The Word of God was a major part of this weeklong Jewish celebration twenty-five hundred years ago. A passion for God was stirred in the hearts of the people when they heard the Word, and the Spirit of God was at work. As a result of this celebration, a genuine revival broke out among the people.

How can it be that the Word can stir our hearts to revival? The Bible is God's Word! They are the words of God to us. According to 2 Timothy 3:16–17, "All Scripture is God-breathed and is useful for teaching, rebuking, correcting and training in righteousness, so that the man of God may be thoroughly equipped for every good work."

The word *breathed* in that verse means inspiration and is referring to the very words themselves. The Word of God is inspired; the words that were written were given by God through human writers. That makes the Bible true, powerful, infallible, and alive. In John 17:17, Jesus said, "Sanctify them by the truth; your Word is *truth*." God's Word is true, and it is also *powerful*. Hebrews 4:12 reads,

> For the word of God is living and active. Sharper than any double-edged sword, it penetrates even to dividing soul and spirit, joints and marrow; it judges the thoughts and attitudes of the heart.

The Word is *infallible*; there is no error. Psalm 18:30, "As for God, his way is perfect; the word of the Lord is flawless." The Word is *alive* and it makes those who open their heart to its offer of salvation alive! Likewise, we read in 1 Thessalonians 2:13,

> …when you received the word of God, which you heard from us, you accepted it not as the word of men, but as it actually is, the word of God, which is at work in you who believe.

The Bible is the only trustworthy authority for faith and life. When Ezra read, the truth found in the Word of God brought joy, and that joy led to a spirit-filled celebration. Remember the words to this song that possibly you sang as a child: "Jesus loves me, this I know, for the Bible tells me so"? Or the "The B-I-B-L-E, yes, that's the book for me!" Both of these songs instill the truth that the Lord loves us and that his Word is our instruction book for life.

The Joy of Celebration Energizes

Well, as we close this chapter know this one thing— God is okay with a time of celebration. Romans 14:17 says, "For the kingdom of God is ... righteousness, and peace, and joy in the Holy Spirit." In Galatians 5:22, we learn about the fruit of the Spirit which is "love, joy, peace, patience, kindness, goodness, faithfulness, gentleness and self-control." Psalm 19:8 tells us, "The precepts of the Lord are right, giving joy to the heart." God endorses celebration. So go ahead, give yourself permission to celebrate something good that has happened in your rebuilding process. Celebration is a time to experience the joy of all that you have accomplished. It's also an opportunity to break away from all of the *doing* and to be refreshed. Once you have experienced a time of celebration, you may want to incorporate regular times of celebration into your life. In a book titled, *Rhythm of Life*, author Richard Exley expresses how vital celebration is for balance in our lives,

Another equally important, but less recognized discipline is the rhythm of life—that delicate balance between work and rest, worship and play. Meaningful work gives our lives definition and purpose. Yet, without a corresponding amount of rest, even creative or spiritual work becomes tedious…Worship and play must then be added to the work/rest cycle to produce the Abundant Life.[10]

Nehemiah 12:27, Jerusalem celebrated "joyfully the dedication with songs of thanksgiving and with music of cymbals, harps, and lyres."

Well, let me finish this chapter by telling you the story of Bunn's burger dance. It was late on Saturday night, after the events of the day, during our January celebration. Just a handful of people were still at the church cleaning up after the meal and fireworks. We were all beginning to head home when one of our elders, David Bunn, stretched himself a bit beyond what was normal for him. Earlier that night, a group of men had barbequed hamburgers on the grill for the meal prior to the service and fireworks. David was walking through the sanctuary with his burger spatula in his hand when someone said, "Whatcha doin', Bunn?"

David stopped and said, "I'm taking my *hamburger flipper* back home."

Then, someone said, "Show us how you flipped those burgers tonight, Bunn." Then, without any hesitation, David started dancing around and acting like he was flipping burgers on the grill—he was truly happy.

Let me tell you, that handful of people who were there, Pam and me included, started laughing. We were laughing so hard that some of us actually fell on the floor as David continued to do his burger dance.

I hope you don't get the wrong impression. This was not an irreligious time at all; instead, it was truly a spiritual moment. The joy of the Lord was the prompter. I think in those few minutes we all felt like the agony and pain of the past fourteen months was worth it. We were so energized from our three-day celebration that if it was necessary, we could have rolled up our sleeves and continued on for another fourteen months.

God is great! God is good! To God be the glory for all the things he has done.

As you can see, the pause for celebration really does prepare us for moving out again in what might be next. Being a part of a celebration really does energize us. Celebration also brings about reflection, and during the time of reflection, we have an opportunity to respond to God with change in our lives and praise. The other part of reflection is to look within and realize the wonderful work that God has done in us when we've made it through our crisis. Now is the time to determine the kind of person we want to be in the days ahead. The next chapter will help us see the importance of becoming the kind of person we need to be.

What Kind of People Should We Be Now?

Day after day, from the first day to the last, Ezra read from the Book of the Law of God. They celebrated the feast for seven days, and on the eighth day, in accordance with the regulation, there was an assembly. On the twenty-fourth day of the same month, the Israelites gathered together, fasting and wearing sackcloth and having dust on their heads.

Nehemiah 8:18, 9:1

Responses to God's Blessings

"Day after day, from the first day to the last … they celebrated" (8:18). The people who had rebuilt the wall, being energized from their celebration, were now ready to move on to what was next. We discover in chapters nine and ten of Nehemiah that the people began to spend some time reflecting on the kind of person they should be, now that the wall was rebuilt. They realized that God had done so much for them, so what was their response to be in return?

They prayed and sought God for the answer. Their seeking was so intense that the Bible says they "gathered together, fasting, and wearing sackcloth and having dust on their heads" (9:1). You might say that they were serious about seeking God for what was next in their lives!

In the three months that it took them to rebuild the wall, they had experienced God in incredible ways. They had experienced his power, his provision, and his protection. The rebuilding led to renewal and celebration, and they wanted more. Their desire for more wasn't about selfish ambitions; they had figured out what life is all about. They were ready for commitment and change. They'd risen above the physical realm where we so often spend our time. They had experienced God in a whole new spiritual way!

In Nehemiah chapters nine and ten, the people review their history in a public gathering. It was a time of counting their blessings. Then we find them making some important promises about things they had come to realize as essential in rising to that spiritual plane where they desired to be. Their spiritual renewal led them to revival—revival in the purest sense of the word; it was as if they were truly living again.

In reviewing their history, they were reminded of the goodness of God over the years. They were riveted with the reality of how awesome God is by saying, "You are the Lord God" (9:7). "You have kept your promise because you are righteous" (9:8). "You sent miraculous signs" (9:10). "You divided the sea" (9:11). "You came down to Mount Sinai" (9:13). "You are a forgiving God, gracious and compassionate; slow to anger and abounding in love" (9:17).

Then, at the end of the ninth chapter, the people came to this conclusion:

> Now therefore, O our God, the great, mighty and awesome God, who keeps his covenant of love, do not let all this hardship seem trifling in your eyes— the hardship that has come upon us, upon our kings and leaders, upon our priests and prophets, upon our fathers and all your people, from the days of the kings of Assyria until today. In all that has happened to us you have been just; you have acted faithfully, while we did wrong.
>
> Nehemiah 9:32–33

They had arrived at an important place of decision-making. They were ready to commit to change in their lives.

Because they realized, beyond a shadow of a doubt, that God was committed to them, they were beginning to grasp the importance of mirroring that same level of commitment to him—"God, who keeps his covenant of love" (9:32). Do you remember Nehemiah's first prayer in chapter one, verse five, "O Lord, God of heaven, the great and awesome God, who keeps his covenant of love"? Here's the exciting thing—the people in Nehemiah's day had come full circle with the reality of God's faithfulness.

It may yet seem impossible to believe, particularly depending on where you are in your crisis and rebuilding process, but your disaster can lead you to that deeper plane of spiritual living. If you want it, that is. If you follow God's example of commitment. God keeps his commitment of love to us—the question is what is our commitment to him?

But you say, "They were under the Law and 'Christ redeemed us from the curse of the law by becoming a curse for us'" (Galatians 3:13). This is true; however, in Galatians 5:13, we read, "You, my brothers, were called to be free. But do not use your freedom to indulge the sinful nature; rather, serve one another in love."

Our commitment to how we will respond to God's blessings and how we intend to live our lives is how we express our love back to God. It is like a couple in a marriage ceremony expressing their love and commitment to each other with their marriage vows. In John 14:15, Jesus said, "If you love me, you will obey what I command."

What was it that the people of Israel committed to after their rebuilding? Can we commit to these same promises to God right now in our lives?

Go–Grow–Gather–Give

I'm not going to preach a sermon, but let me give you an alliterated outline of what is found in this passage of Nehemiah with these words: *go—grow—gather—give*. We find each of these four points in chapter ten of Nehemiah. These four words represent our response to God for his blessings to us and the way we want to live our lives.

First, we see that the people that Nehemiah worked with made a commitment "to obey carefully all the commands, regulations and decrees of the Lord our Lord" (10:29). This represents the *go* of the outline. To obey means take action, and that means *go*. It's one thing to know what we need to do, but to do it is another thing. In the New Testament, James 2:17 says, "In the same way, faith by itself, if it is not accompanied by action, is dead." How can your commitment to God be expressed by action, obedience, and the word *go*?

The next word, *grow*, is reflected in these words. They "separated themselves from the neighboring peoples" (10:28), and they said, "We promise not to give our daughters in marriage to the peoples around us" (10:30). The Jewish people were to be a distinct people modeling separation from the world. For us, separation from the world is expressed in our dedication to God. Dedication is all about *growing*. Jesus said, "…you do not belong to the world, but I have chosen you out of the world" (John 15:19). Paul commented about the new believers in Thessalonica saying, "You turned to God from idols to serve the living and true God" (1 Thessalonians 1:9). And in Romans 12:1–2, we read,

> Therefore, I urge you, brothers, in view of God's mercy, to offer your bodies as living sacrifices, holy and pleasing to God—this is your spiritual act of worship. Do not conform any longer to the pattern of this world, but be transformed by the renewing of your mind.

What is God saying to you about dedication to him and your commitment to *grow*?

Nehemiah 10:31 is about honoring the Sabbath—

> When the neighboring peoples bring merchandise
> or grain to sell on the Sabbath, we will not buy
> from them on the Sabbath or on any holy day.
> Every seventh year, we will forgo working the land
> and will cancel all debts.

Today, we *gather* on Sunday as Christians because of
the resurrection of Christ. Christ arose from the grave
on the first day of the week. This pattern for gathering
began with the early church as recorded in the book
of Acts. How much do we let other things get in our
way of observing the Sabbath by *gathering* together on
Sunday?

> And let us consider how we may spur one another
> on toward love and good deeds. Let us not give up
> meeting together, as some are in the habit of doing,
> but let us encourage one another—and all the more
> as you see the Day approaching.
>
> Hebrews 10:24–25

What's your habit? Do you *gather* regularly with other
believers?

For the ministries of God to exist, it requires the
support of his people—*giving*. Next in chapter ten, we
read, "…the Levites when they receive the tithes…are
to bring a tenth of the tithes up to the house of our God"
(10:38). The people take on the responsibility for carrying
out the commands to give. Then in the next verse, it says,
"The people…are to bring their contributions of grain,
new wine and oil to the storerooms" (10:39). Then the
people said, "We will not neglect the house of our God"

(10:39). The people were committed to *give*. When we hear the word *giving*, our minds almost immediately go to money. Granted giving is about money; however, God is more interested in our heart than our wallet. God owns "the cattle on a thousand hills" (Psalm 50:10). Everything is his. He has need of nothing. Actually the only thing he may not have is our heart. To give our heart is a choice he lets us make. *Giving* is about our treasure, our talent, and our time. What is your commitment to God about *giving*?

Commitment Requires Change

Making such commitments requires change. Change is hard and maybe that's why we so often find ourselves breaking commitments. What can we learn about change? Have you ever traded for a newer car after driving one for a number of years? Were all the knobs and controls in different places? If so, how long did you keep turning on the wipers when you wanted to set the cruise control? Habits are hard to change. In the same way we can get too comfortable with where we are in our relationship with God.

Granted, some things should not change. "Stand at the crossroads and look; ask for the ancient paths, ask where the good way is, and walk in it, and you will find rest for your souls" (Jeremiah 6:16). In the New Testament, Paul says, "...hold firmly to the trustworthy message as it has been taught, so that he can encourage others by sound doctrine and refute those who oppose it" (Titus 1:9).

Some things don't change; however, there are things that should change—and that change starts with us. "Therefore, if anyone is in Christ, he is a new creation; the old has gone, the new has come!" (2 Corinthians 5:17). Noah had to change his life to build the ark. Abram had to pack up and travel to a new land to be the father of a new nation. Moses and David had to give up shepherding in order to obey God. Jonah had to wrestle with a major prejudice he had in order to obey God. Peter, Andrew, James, and John had to leave behind a fishing business. Saul had to let go of deeply held beliefs and change his life totally to obey God.

All these examples are about change. Change is not always necessary, but appropriate change is vital when it comes to following God! " ... any of you who does not give up everything he has cannot be my disciple" (Luke 14:33). Paul admonishes us to " ... not conform any longer to the pattern of this world, but be transformed by the renewing of your mind" (Romans 12:2). So then, " ... we, who with unveiled faces all reflect the Lord's glory, are being transformed into his likeness with ever-increasing glory, which comes from the Lord, who is the Spirit" (2 Corinthians 3:18).

God is a commitment maker and a commitment keeper. You may have made some promises to God in the past that you haven't kept because it was hard to change. If that is so, you're not alone. Don't let that keep you from making those commitments to change, again. In Jeremiah, God says, that " ... they broke my covenant, though I was a husband to them" (31:32). Then in the next verse, we learn that God did not give up on them by saying, "I will put my law in their minds and write it on their hearts. I will be their God, and they will be my people" (31:33).

The Katrina stories for this chapter are still being

written. The message of the stories will depend on our response to God's blessings. What will our level of commitment be? How will we express our love and *go—grow—gather—give?*

These words are an encouragement for us to be the kind of person we should be: "For the eyes of the Lord range throughout the earth to strengthen those whose hearts are fully committed to him" (2 Chronicles 16:9).

This brings us to the final chapter. I outlined the chapters of this book one year after Katrina, and at that time there were ten chapters. Now that we're further along with our journey, the next chapter has immerged asking a question. Where do we go from here? We are discovering the answer to this question several years after our disaster.

Where Do We Go from Here?

> For it is by grace you have been saved, through faith—and this not from yourselves, it is the gift of God—not by works, so that no one can boast. For we are God's workmanship, created in Christ Jesus to do good works, which God prepared in advance for us to do.
>
> Ephesians 2:8–10

So much has been accomplished since Hurricane Katrina; we have seen a lot of amazing and wonderful things. The rebuilding efforts that have occurred have been unbelievable along the Mississippi Gulf Coast, and yet, there has been a sense that there is so much more to do. Out of our church's initiatives, we have accomplished over two hundred cleanup projects, repaired our church facility, and numerous volunteer crews have completed over eighty home-rebuilding projects for our church families and in our outreach phase to others.

We also had an opportunity to pay it forward, by helping our sister church in New Orleans—Iglesia Amor Viviente. In January 2007, Amor Viviente still had need of help with repairs to their church building, and they still had fifteen families that were not back in their homes. Having that information, we began to route volunteer crews from churches that continued to call us about coming to the Gulf Coast to Amor Viviente. We also gave out of our church's relief fund, seed money for their relief efforts. Pastor Karl Bernhard, his wife, Marlene, and Blanca Mackay persevered and were overcomers during this time. They provided great leadership to their congregation; and their church initiative blessed the congregation as well as serving others through outreach opportunities.

All along the way on our rebuilding journey, God revealed himself in a variety of ways. Because of the disaster and crisis that followed, we were now like a tire with a slow leak. It took some time; but we began to realize that besides the material damages, Katrina had taken a toll on each of us personally and we were suffering from Katrina fatigue. Fortunately, ever so often, we would have a God moment that seemed to come along at just the right time, filling us with a sense of hope for the future.

One such moment occurred seven weeks after Katrina and served as a continual reminder of hope. The hurricane winds had not only destroyed many structures, it had also stripped away all of the vegetation across the Gulf Coast. Flowers and leaves on trees and bushes were completely gone. What was once green now looked dead. Needless to say, this drastic change in the scenery created a negative and discouraging effect on everyone who went through the storm.

Then one day, during the first part of October 2005, a green cast started to appear on the trees. The same was true for the bushes and other plants in the area. Amazingly, things were starting to grow again. Plants and trees that seemed dead were coming alive!

One day, I stopped by to check on a couple from our church, Tom and Peggy Ward. I wasn't at their house long when Peggy said she wanted to show me something. As we were walking, I could see that she was leading me to several rose bushes in her yard. These rose bushes had been stripped to the stem, but now they were covered with green leaves and beautiful roses. It wasn't spring, but those rose bushes were flowering again. For all of us, this was evidence that there was new life springing out of all of the death and destruction around us. I have seen it with my own eyes; God does give us "beauty instead of ashes" (Isaiah 61:3)— good things can and will come out of bad circumstances when we have right responses.

> … to comfort all who mourn, and provide for those who grieve in Zion—to bestow on them a crown of beauty instead of ashes, the oil of gladness instead of mourning, and a garment of praise instead of a spirit of despair. They will be called oaks of righteousness, a planting of the Lord for the display of his splendor.
>
> Isaiah 61:2–3

One day, I was having breakfast with one of the volunteer teams at the church and was sharing this story of how adversity caused the flowers to bloom even out of their normal seasonal cycle. Sitting next to me was an Amish buggy maker, from Pennsylvania, who was intrigued by what I was saying. He then told me,

> I've done something similar to fruit trees that won't produce. I wrap the trunk with burlap and beat it with a baseball bat until I'm exhausted. Amazingly, later, that tree will bloom and produce fruit because of the stress that was created.

Wow, a couple of questions immediately come to my mind, Could all of what we were going through have a strengthening and fruitful result? Is there a harvest yet to come?

Rebuilding is Not an End, but Rather a Means To an End

Gene and Patty Gardner, friends from Illinois, came to stay with us in January of 2006. They helped with projects that volunteer teams were working on, but beyond that, they stayed in our home, and during those three weeks, they personally encouraged Pam and me. They helped us break away from the work and have some fun. It may have been the first time that we had laughed since the storm. Before they left, they gave us an incredible picture as a gift. It now hangs in my office at the church. It's a painting of a lighthouse in a storm with waves splashing against the structure. When you look closely, you see a man standing on the ledge outside of the lighthouse door in the middle of the storm. There is a Scripture verse etched at the bottom from Psalm 18:2, "The Lord is my rock, my fortress and my deliverer; my God is my rock, in whom I take refuge." We still have our ups and downs from time to time, and there are times, even now, when the gaps between laughter are too long. Though there are still questions that come up about what's next and what we still need. Their gift is a constant reminder of why we are where we are! Could it be that greater things are yet to come?

Marcus Smucker was another person that came along at the right time. Marcus provided pastoral care to Pam and me from time to time over the period of a year. After all, who can a pastor and his wife go to when they are going through a major disaster? We learned quickly that having someone like Marcus to go to with a listening ear and understanding heart is essential and beneficial during a crisis. Marcus was a sounding board for us, helping us process things we were thinking and feeling. He helped us keep things in perspective, our sights on the future and the good that could possibly come out of our disaster.

Have you ever had a time in your life when something just didn't seem right? Maybe, it felt as if you were walking out of step. Well, that's what has been going on along the Gulf Coast. Even though a lot has been accomplished since Katrina and, for the most part, things are actually improved over the way they were, there has been this unexplainable dynamic going on. I'm not sure that it would be categorized as post-traumatic stress syndrome, but there is definitely some emotional or psychological phenomenon happening with many of the folks who live along the Gulf Cost.

As you may recall, the summer of 2008 was another very active hurricane season, and Hurricanes Gustav and Ike were two of the major hurricanes that were threatening the Gulf Coast region. Thankfully, the outcome was that neither Gustav nor Ike was as devastating as Katrina for those of us that live in south Mississippi. But the reality is that those two hurricanes revealed so much anxiety in the people that it became apparent that we are not completely over the effects of Hurricane Katrina. During the days leading up to the landfall of those two storms, the anxiety was so high that I heard someone say, "You could have cut the tension with a knife."

Lifelong residents of south Mississippi were saying, "I'm not ready for this, again. If we experience another Katrina, I'll be ready to move far away from the Gulf Coast."

What became apparent was the fact that Hurricanes Gustav and Ike were revealing where the people of the Gulf Coast were emotionally. We may have moved beyond much of the structural damage, but there is still a lot of work to be done in the area of restoring people's lives. These responses are very real. The people along the Gulf Coast have lost a lot, and things will never be exactly the same as they were before. It is only to be expected that the people along the Gulf Coast would be affected in the way they live, work, and worship by the stresses they have experienced from Hurricane Katrina.

In our ministry, we worked with people who were frustrated, tired, and on the verge of burnout. Discouragement was not an uncommon factor in the lives of most of the people along the Gulf Coast. People would say, "My house has been rebuilt. It's even better than it was before, so why do I feel so discouraged?" Some of the people along the Gulf Coast would actually feel guilty because they were so discouraged. They would try to reason with themselves, saying, "Why should I feel this way? After all, look at all that has been done for me." When in actuality, for some folks, that added to their thoughts of guilt. They felt that they did not deserve what was being done for them or they felt guilty that they were being helped.

The Beginning of a New Ministry

For us, it has become apparent that there is another kind of rebuilding that is needed along the Mississippi Gulf Coast. It's a rebuilding of lives. As a result of all this, my wife, Pam, and I are developing an effort to help rebuild people's lives. We've incorporated and have received non-profit status for a ministry that is called Relevant Ministry (www.relevantministry.org). I had been using that name for a ministry that originally was established as a Website to encourage people to find their *right fit* in spiritual gifts-based ministry.

Today, Relevant Ministry has broadened its vision to train future leaders and to help build back healthy churches and ministries. Our church lost fifty-seven of it members and regular attendees who for one reason or another moved out of the area because of the storm. Such losses, along with all the disaster response efforts, has had a major impact on current ministry programs not only in our church, but all along the Gulf Coast.

Just as folks came from outside our area to help us rebuild our homes, businesses, and church buildings, the initiatives of Relevant Ministry hopefully will help to bring about a much needed spiritual rebuilding. Our hope is that, over the next four to five years, restored church leaders along the Coast will be revived spiritually and that Katrina fatigued ministries will become healthy again.

Two Coastal Icons Are a Picture of the Future

As an illustration of the mission of Relevant Ministry to the Gulf Coast, I would like to share with you two stories about important landmarks that are situated along our shoreline on Beach Boulevard.

Immediately after Katrina, people were beginning to ask about the outcome of two of our most famous landmarks—the Biloxi Lighthouse and the Friendship Tree. Everyone wanted to know what kind of storm damage they had and if they were still standing.

Like everything else in Katrina's path, they were affected by the wind and the water surge. Both the lighthouse and the old oak tree had made it through the storm; but not without incident. Both of these famous landmarks needed to be repaired.

Somehow, just knowing that the Biloxi Lighthouse and the Friendship Tree in Long Beach survived the storm, people had a sense of relief and hope for the future. That lighthouse has stood along those shores since 1848, and it was truly a part of the Gulf Coast's identity.

The lighthouse did have to undergo some major

repairs, but it is still standing. The lighthouse has become such a symbol of hope that it has replaced our state flower, the magnolia, on our Mississippi license plates for our vehicles. And a postage stamp came out in the summer of 2009 displaying the image of the Biloxi Lighthouse.[11]

And the Friendship Tree, well, it has weathered many storms in its five hundred-plus-year history. This enormous live oak with the branch foliage spread of 156 feet has made the campus of the University of Southern Mississippi Gulf Park Campus a famous place.[12] The tree is so fascinating because some of the branches actually grow down, touch the ground, and grow back up again. The Friendship Tree truly is a stopping place for locals and visitors alike, who stand in amazement under its canopy of hanging moss and ferns that grow out of its limbs.

Although the Friendship Tree had storm damage, it is still standing—standing but not as strong as it once was. The tree house-style platform that visitors used to climb up into near the trunk of the tree has not been replaced. Currently, there is a sign that says that the tree is still recovering and that it is not strong enough to sustain any extra weight. Even today, the Friendship Tree is being undergirded by wooden stilts that have been built to support the weakened branches. Of course, everyone's hope is that some day adults and children will be able to climb on its limbs and go up into the branches to see the beautiful Gulf from its vantage point once again.

Wouldn't it be wonderful if that same hope could be extended to the ministries along the Gulf Coast that have weathered the storm? Suppose for a moment that ministries became stronger because of the support that they may receive in a time of need. Imagine the opportunities that a church or ministry might have to bring the timeless truths of God alive in new and exciting ways. Just picture a church or ministry modeling care and compassion out of their own experiences in fresh and relevant ways.

So where do we go from here? Could the nation's worst natural disaster turn out to be a blessing? Did God have plans beyond what we were able to see during our crisis? Could his plans be above and beyond what we could ever ask or hope for? Is it possible that there is yet a harvest to come along the Gulf Coast?

And, so let me ask you, where do you go from here? Could your disaster turn out to be a blessing? Does God have plans beyond what you are able to see? Could his plans be above and beyond what you could ever ask or hope for?

Chris Tomlin sings about that future vision of greater things in the song, "God of This City":

> You're the God of this city
> You're the King of these people
> You're the Lord of this nation
> You are
> You're the Light in this darkness
> You're the Hope to the hopeless
> You're the Peace to the restless
> You are
> There is no one like our God
> There is no one like our God
> For greater things have yet to come

Where Do We Go from Here?

And greater things are still to be done in this city
Greater things have yet to come
And greater things are still to be done here[13]

For us, our sustaining relationship with God, the encouragement that we received from the principles in Nehemiah, the support that we felt from first responders and volunteers, and the sense of community that we have gained in our congregation has paved a way to choose a path of resiliency into the future. We are looking to the greater things that are yet to come.

Appendix I
How to Develop a Local Church Disaster Response Ministry

This section of the book, *Nehemiah Response*, has been written specifically for churches and ministries to advocate a disaster preparedness plan that includes a disaster response ministry. Should a disaster strike, most businesses today have a contingency plan in place. This is a well thought-out plan, prepared in advance should a disaster affect their business' operation. This advanced planning is about having important decisions made prior to the actual event.

There are two important parts of disaster preparedness to consider for a church and ministry. The first part is being ready for the event and being protected. The second is being ready to respond to ministry opportunities. For businesses, this second part is getting back as soon as possible, doing what they do during normal daily operations. I want to encourage you to be thinking about the importance of your church and ministry being ready to respond with ministry as soon as possible after a disaster. Do you have such a disaster plan in place? What might it mean to you and to your ministry area if you had a disaster plan should a disaster strike? Begin asking the following questions: What would we do in an emergency? And what responsibilities will certain people have if a disaster strikes?

As a result of our Katrina experience, we discovered firsthand the ministry opportunities following a disaster. We were not ready and had to move quickly to respond to the door that God was opening. Here are important questions that we need to ask ourselves in order to begin thinking ahead like this: How likely is it that an emergency would strike in our area? What kind of disaster could there be? How can we be ready to serve and seize opportunities for ministry that would arise? The church can respond uniquely like this in any disaster. The church is the body of Christ. Collectively, the church has within its participants the skills, talents, and spiritual gifts to meet many of the needs that arise out of a disaster. The church is made up of people who, if properly mobilized, can further the kingdom carrying out the Great Commandment and the Great Commission when a disaster hits their area.

You may never experience a hurricane because you live somewhere other than near the Coast or ocean shores; however, disasters are more than hurricanes. A disaster can be anything that disrupts life and normal activity—tornadoes, earthquakes, mudslides, winter storms, floods, fires, etc. Because we are living in such uncertain times, it seems that these types of natural disasters along with terrorists' threats have intensified. I'm not being an alarmist; rather I'm being a realist. As Christians, we don't need to be afraid of these things; but it is important to be ready.

If a disaster hit in the area where you are serving, could your church and its members (1) sustain yourself in that emergency, and (2) would you be able to respond to possible ministry opportunities of helping, serving, and reaching out?

Granted, most denominations have a disaster agency on the national level that will respond. These national agencies are important and their mission and response is vital. However, what we experienced as a local church following Katrina is that unique opportunities present themselves by being right in the middle of that disaster. Fortunately, our church was able to make a quick response. We were there, and we could identify with the needs of the area because we had experienced the storm. It didn't take us several months to move into the area, set up, and begin an operation. The necessary assets to begin were already in place, because our church had people that were ready and willing to serve and we had a place to operate out of. We were already familiar with our ministry area. We were uniquely positioned. Local, grass roots initiatives can be very effective. What the large agencies do is needed and meaningful, and productive responses can be collaborated.

Ministry is why the church exists; however, responding to a catastrophic, natural disaster is certainly ministry in a whole new way. Because we were able to think outside of the box at the time of Katrina, our response to this disaster became an important ministry just like our men's ministry, music ministry, young married ministry, or any other ministry that we were more familiar with.

So let me encourage you to consider starting a disaster response ministry in your church. Are you the pastor or a leader in a church? Are you the entrepreneur type? Are you able to see the possibility of a new ministry and have the ability to share that vision with others? If so, on the following pages I will give you some steps that might help you to get the ball rolling in your ministry.

Here's an example of something that helped open our eyes to see the need for preparedness. It came out of the need to communicate with church members following Katrina. Although I had been in the ministry full time for over thirty-five years, a communication plan following a disaster was not something that I had even considered putting into place. Immediately after the storm passed, as a pastor to a congregation, I felt such a responsibility to connect with all the members of our church to see how they were doing. Unfortunately, there was no system in place at that time. Three years later, when it looked like Gustav and Ike could be coming our way, we instituted a communication system as part of our preparedness plan. We now have a simple predetermined system of checking in both before and after a possible disaster. Just knowing that we have a way to account for everyone in our congregation brings relief to the leadership. People of the congregation have responded positively and they also feel cared for. One person commented when they checked in after Gustav by saying, "This contact site is a great idea. Thanks for thinking of it."

If your church does not have a disaster preparedness plan, let me get you started. It would be impossible for me to write your preparedness plan, but you
can. Your plan may be different from our church's
plan or any other church's plan for that matter. Your
plan will need to be unique to your area—its weather,
environment, etc. In the following sections, I will
walk you through some advanced steps to help you
develop your preparedness plan.

First things first: If you feel that the Lord is putting
the need to develop a preparedness plan on your heart,
you will want to begin by sharing your vision with key
people in your church. Whatever your church govern-
mental policies are, you will want to abide with them
before you get started.

Once you have your okay to start, I would rec-
ommend that you and others read through *Nehemiah
Response* together to lay the groundwork for your disaster response ministry. As you go through our church's
story and Nehemiah's response to a disaster, try to
put yourself in the storyline. Think about what you
would do, who would be responsible for certain areas
of need, and what would be essential to have in place
for each stage of a rebuilding process. You may want to
make plans for this group of interested people to meet
together possibly in a short-term small group, focus
group, or Sunday school class.

Facilitating a disaster response ministry group: During
the first meeting of your group, find out why each person is interested in being a part of the disaster response
ministry. As you continue to meet, the participants of
the group will begin to discover their different niches
and roles on the team. Also in the first meeting put a

plan together for reading through *Nehemiah Response* over the next ten to twelve weeks. Before you dismiss, determine when you're meetings will be and for how long. To fully develop a preparedness plan, it will probably take the full ten to twelve weeks that you have planned to go through the book.

In your next meeting, take time to discuss the book *Nehemiah Response*. Continue discussion about possible roles and niches for the different members of the group. Consider taking a spiritual gift assessment, you may have one you use, if you are in need of a resource there is some instruction and an online assessment on the Relevant Ministry Website—www.relevantministry.org. The results could be very helpful for the group as you are forming. Also on that same Website, you will find some pointers for starting a new ministry that your group may want to consider.

During the second or third meeting give everyone an assignment to do some research on preparedness. There is a wealth of up-to-date information that you can find online. Here are Websites to definitely consider for your research information:

Homeland Security—www.ready.gov

The U. S. Department of Homeland Security, in partnership with the Advertising Council, has a Website that advocates readiness. This Website has good information to educate individuals about preparation and responses to all kinds of emergencies. The Ready Campaign asks individuals to do three key things to prepare for the unexpected: get an emergency supply kit, make a family emergency plan, and be informed about the different types of emergencies that could occur and appropriate responses to those emergences. Whoever is researching this Website can apply this information for your church as a larger group.

The Red Cross—www.redcross.org and www.prepare.org
The American Red Cross information, like the Homeland Security Website, focuses on individual preparedness. Both Websites will stimulate the group's thinking for ministry planning. The Red Cross Website informs us that a "disaster can strike quickly and without warning." People can be forced to evacuate or they may be confined to their home in an emergency. The Website asks what you would do if basic services—water, gas, electricity, or telephone were cut off.

Sesame Workshop—www.sesameworkshop.org
When Hurricane Katrina devastated the Gulf Coast in August 2005, Sesame Workshop resulted from early responders with clothing, food, and toys for children. Today the workshop offers children social and emotional support for dealing with the trauma of disaster. This Website will stimulate thinking about ministering to the needs of youth and children following a disaster event.

Federal Emergency Management Agency (FEMA)— www.fema.gov
www.fema.gov/areyouready is a link on the FEMA Website with a section titled "Are You Ready?" The information here is an in-depth guide to preparedness. There is a step-by-step approach to disaster preparedness that will help your team to get informed about local emergency plans, how to identify hazards that affect your

local area; and how to develop and maintain an emergency communication plan and disaster supplies. Other topics covered include evacuation, emergency public shelters, animals in disaster, and information specific to people with disabilities.

Mississippi Emergency Management Agency (MEMA)—www.msema.org

Mississippi's government leaders, beginning with our governor—Haley Barbour—and the state's agencies did a stellar job of responding to the needs of people in the aftermath of Katrina. From that experience so many more things were learned. This Website offers a wealth of practical, on-target information that has come out of Mississippians' practical experience. (Also see your state's Homeland Security office's Website that is linked to the U. S. Department of Homeland Security Website.)

On the following five Websites there are manuals and information related to business preparation—www.sba.gov, www.fema.gov, www.prepare.org, www.ibhs.org, www.nfib.com. As you research and read over these materials your group will be able to make application to your church's preparedness plan and disaster response ministry.

Links to these Websites and other information can be found on the Nehemiah Response Website (www.nehemiahresponse.com)—click the *Preparedness* link—for this and additional information. I would suggest that you check these pages online regularly throughout your group's planning time for the latest information. For additional dialogue about preparedness, you will find web pages dedicated to this topic under the *Preparedness* link on the Nehemiah Response Website. You can post information that you are discovering and also receive information from others that may be helpful for you. I believe that you will find that collaboration and networking is a key part for starting and developing this type of ministry since it is in its infancy in the area of church ministry.

As your group continues to meet, let me encourage you to not get overwhelmed with all the information you are gathering. Sift through it, identifying what is most important for your situation, and then begin to assign someone to be responsible for each part or action. Remember to draw from your resources by implementing what your group discovered through the spiritual gifts assessment. Remember, this is a new process, so incorporate flexibility and keep working at it; soon your response team will clearly emerge and your disaster response ministry will be launched and ready.

Here are some questions for your group to consider in the planning meetings:

> How prepared are we?
>
> Do we need hazard insurance?
>
> Are we prepared to relocate temporarily?
>
> What would our congregation do if we could not meet at our building?
>
> Is each family of our congregation prepared for possible disaster?
>
> Do our fire extinguishers work?

Do we need to have a safety drill for a worship gathering?

Are vital records protected?

Do we have copies and immediate access to vital records?

Is there a communication plan in place that everyone knows about?

Do we have some emergency funds available?

What is our fundraising capacity?

What connections do we have with other ministries outside our area?

Who are the national disaster response groups we are associated with?

What are the policies of these national groups that guide their response strategy?

The following are lists for individuals and families, from www.ready.gov to be familiar with and for your ministry group to think through at a congregational level and shape for your church's needs:

Basic Emergency Supply Kit:

1. One gallon of water per person per day for three days

2. Food for your family for three days

3. Battery-powered radio

4. NOAA Weather Radio with tone alert

5. Flashlight
6. Extra batteries
7. First aid kit
8. Pet food and water

Specialized Emergency Supply Kit

1. At least three days' supply of medicines or medical treatments
2. Important documents
3. Copy of prescriptions, dosage, and treatment information
4. Eyeglasses, hearing aids and batteries, wheelchair batteries, oxygen
5. Copies of medical insurance, Medicare and Medicaid cards
6. Information on any equipment or lifesaving devices you use

Basic Family Emergency Plan:

1. Contact numbers - local and out-of-area
2. Meeting locations - local and out-of-area
3. Date of birth, social security information, and medical information
4. School and workplace emergency plans

In your final two or three meetings, your disaster response ministry team will want to categorize its findings and plans into these three segments of disaster preparedness and response as they begin to write their plan.

1. *Prior to disaster*: The most important thing you may do besides prepare is to share your preparedness plan with your congregation. Your plan is about prevention, mitigation where possible, and responses you will make in an emergency.

2. *During a disaster*: This is when you benefit from your readiness and preparedness. This is where you protect and sustain yourself during your emergency.

3. *After a disaster*: Most disaster agencies define this time in three stages: rescuing (days), resuming (weeks and months), and rebuilding (years). This is about rebuilding and restoration. This is your church's ministry response—what will you do and who will do what. This is where your disaster response ministry springs into action. This is what you got ready for. Here is where your local church as Christ's body responds in Great Commandment and Great Commission ways for the glory of God.

Now, you're ready:

With these steps you will be ready! You are prepared, and maybe your preparation is for something that will never happen, but if an emergency strikes, you will be ready. Because of your advanced action, your team has positioned your church to sustain itself during an emergency, and it will be ready to seize ministry opportunities that follow. (Periodically update your plan, contact lists, and so forth.)

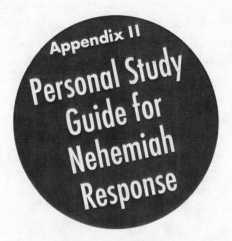

Appendix II

Personal Study Guide for Nehemiah Response

Have you experienced a disaster recently? Your disaster may not be a hurricane, like what we went through, but nonetheless, any situation that brings with it loss has some kind of rebuilding that follows. No matter where you are on your rebuilding journey, I want to encourage you because the crisis that follows a disaster can be turned into an opportunity. Somehow, in God's providence, "we know that in all things God works for the good of those who love him" (Romans 8:28).

The following personal study guide can be a tool to help you think and work through the crisis that your disaster has produced. Obstacles you may face now can be overcome. The challenges of today can shape tomorrow's successes.

Having the Word of God, and particularly the book of Nehemiah, helped all of us at our church work through the aftermath of Hurricane Katrina. Principles from this great, Old Testament book shed light on steps that we could take during our troubled time. These principles worked powerfully for us, not because they were some good idea that we invented, but because they were from God. These principles worked for Nehemiah during his rebuilding time, and I believe that you will find that they can help you, too.

Let me encourage you to establish a study plan that helps you as you go through this personal study guide. It is divided into the same eleven chapter divisions of this book. In each of the eleven sections below, I have put key principles from the chapter and have given you some questions to consider.

If you want to have a more in-depth Bible study, I have provided Website address links to messages from Nehemiah that I preached at my church. This series titled "How to Get to Where I'm Going" was given three years after Katrina. Nehemiah and its timeless principles had as much relevance for us then as it did just months after the storm. It was encouraging for us to see where we had come from and where we were going.

What do you do when something bad strikes? (Chapter 1)

What has happened to you?

Do you feel that it was done to you, or is it something that you are at least partly responsible for?

What has been your response to God up to this point? Have you been running to him or from him?

Are you able to view God as a lifeline?

What can you do to make this connection?

One of the questions asked in this chapter is if you have invited Jesus Christ to become the Lord and Savior of your life. Is that something that you have done at some point in your life or is today the day for you to begin a new life in Christ?

Nehemiah knew God, and he prayed a powerful prayer in Nehemiah chapter one following his realization of the condition of Jerusalem. He said, "...the great and awesome God, who keeps his covenant of love..." (1:5). Know this one thing: God loves you just as much as he loved Nehemiah! Will you include him in your life and experience his promise of love for you?

Audio Message one—"Getting a Clear Vision"
www.nehemiahresponse.com/audio/one.asp

About the audio message: Nehemiah's hope-filled visionary leadership is a powerful example for leaders today. Everybody ends up somewhere in life; however, a few people end up where they do on purpose. The ones that do are the ones with vision.

The most practical advantage of vision is that it sets a direction for our lives. In this message from chapter one of Nehemiah, we learn how to get a clear vision. By listening to this message you will learn more about vision from the experiences of Nehemiah. Vision is often born out of a concern that is caused from the tension between what is and what could be.

So, is there a plan for me in all of this? (Chapter 2)

A principle we learned from Nehemiah is that *action is not necessarily the first response* when a disaster strikes. What did Nehemiah do to keep from reacting to the crises? He stopped and prayed. His first response was to seek out God and see the problem from God's perspective. A tendency we can have is to want to do something right away, to *fix it*.

From this principle, we can see the importance of waiting on God to reveal his plan. If we get too actively involved before we have direction from God, we could miss his idea and leading. Patience is truly a virtue when you are going through a crisis. Remember that God has a purpose and reason for every situation that we go through. "Consider it pure joy, my brothers, whenever you face trials of many kinds, because you know that the testing of your faith develops perseverance. Perseverance must finish its work so that you may be mature and complete, not lacking anything" (James 1:2–4).

What was your first response to your disaster?

Have you stopped and prayed about your situation?

It might be too early in your situation, but can you see God's plan... his purpose... or reason for this situation in your life?

Do you feel isolated or have you made the effort to reach out?

It is critical that you have someone to trust in your life when you are going through a crisis. Who are the people that you have surrounded yourself with?

Instead of a message link for this section, let me encourage you to read Nehemiah's prayer in Nehemiah 1:5–11, if you want to go a little deeper in this study. Notice that Nehemiah not only took time to seek out God, but he also surrounded himself with a few people he could trust.

How do you put a plan together? (Chapter 3)

Three principles immerged from this chapter on planning. Nehemiah rested, he reflected, and then he rallied support or took appropriate action. Because Nehemiah took time to get in step with God he was ready for action when the door of opportunity opened.

Is it hard for you to wait for the right time?

How can you turn your tendency to react into a right action?

Why do you think rest is so important?

Can you name some benefits to resting?

Now, here's the real question: Are you getting enough rest?

Nehemiah fully reflected on all that needed to be done. He researched and got all the facts before he began to work on the wall.

Is there some reflection or research that would help you in your situation?

"To rally" shows action taken in a comeback at a sporting event. What action do you need to take, today?

Audio Message two: "Moving Forward at the Right Time"

www.nehemiahresponse.com/audio/two.asp

About the audio message: The days that Nehemiah spent in prayer could be compared to a time of incubation. During that time, Nehemiah's vision became clearer, and out of an intense time spent in prayer, the plan came together. With this analogy of incubation, we can understand the importance of moving forward at the right time. What were some of the things that Nehemiah did during this time of incubation? What can we learn? What are the transferable principles that we can use in our lives today? How can we be sure we are moving forward at the right time?

Audio Message three: "How to Implement the Vision" part 1

www.nehemiahresponse.com/audio/three.asp

About the audio message: Without taking action–vision is just a dream. In the last half of the second chapter of Nehemiah, we discover his strategy for action. From the things we see him doing, we can develop transferable principles that can work in our own setting. Listening to this message will help you to learn how to get to where we are going.

Audio Message four: "How to Implement the Vision" part 2

www.nehemiahresponse.com/audio/four.asp

About the audio message: Morale in Jerusalem was at an all-time low when Nehemiah implemented the vision to rebuild the wall. Residents of the city could have been skeptical because of discouragement. They could have wondered, "Who is this guy?" They could have questioned, "Who does he think he is?" However, the time was right, and Nehemiah was carefully in sync with God. So, what can we learn about implementing a vision that God has given to us? What is transferable from Nehemiah's success to our situation?

Audio Message five: "The Hand of God"

www.nehemiahresponse.com/audio/five.asp

About the audio message: Nehemiah had clarified the vision from God to rebuild the wall of Jerusalem. He had taken time for the plan to come together. We called that a time of incubation. In the second chapter, he had begun implementation. He had taken action. This is the same process for us for any initiative that God calls us to.

We see Nehemiah highly involved. In Nehemiah 2:18, Nehemiah points out another essential aspect that we cannot overlook; God had a plan—it was God's idea. When we realize this, we will be able to see two important factors for any kingdom mission: the sovereignty of God and the responsibility of man. These two factors should be in perfect balance.

Twice in chapter two, Nehemiah says that the hand of God is on him. This message takes a look at what this means and also how we can be sure that the hand of God is on us.

What's this about fear? (Chapter 4)

Fear is something that can grip us and keep us from action. Recognizing God's provision for our needs can calm our fears and strengthen our faith.

What are you afraid of today?

What would you do if you were not afraid?

What type of fear arises when you think about moving out?

How do you see God providing for you?

How are your fears being overcome by God's provision for you?

Do you have the realization that God will take care of you?

Dig a little deeper in the book of Nehemiah by reading Nehemiah's response to his employer, the king (2:1–8). Notice Nehemiah's fear in the beginning. See the king's response back to Nehemiah when Nehemiah pressed through his fears.

How do you put your plan into action? (Chapter 5)

We leaned three strategies in this chapter where Nehemiah put the plan into action. The strategies involved prioritizing, working as teams, and working from the inside-out: beginning where you are and moving out.

What are all the things that you need to accomplish?

Have you stopped to prioritize your steps?

Nehemiah took the concept of prioritizing a little further. His emphasis was on *who's* first over *what's* first.

What does that mean to you?

How do you make God first? Is he in the center of your life?

What are the benefits of working as a team?

What makes working in a team difficult?

Is it hard for you to receive help from others?

How open are you to receiving, not only help, but also advice from someone else?

How does the inside-out principle apply to you and your situation?

Audio Message six: "Strategy That Works" part 1
www.nehemiahresponse.com/audio/six.asp
    About the audio message: Strategy answers the following questions: What should you be doing to get to where you are going? How can I arrive at my desired outcome?

Strategy is a Greek word that means *generalship*. So strategy is what leads us to where we are going.

In the third chapter of Nehemiah, we find three key action steps that led up to accomplishing the goal of rebuilding the wall in Jerusalem. These same actions are transferable to your situation. After you know where you are going, these major strategies will fit your situation. You can check them out by listening to this message.

Audio Message seven: "Strategy That Works" part 2
www.nehemiahresponse.com/audio/seven.asp

About the audio message: Jerusalem was in great need of repair; the wall was broken down and the gates were destroyed; however, God had another plan for Jerusalem. His desire was for the city to be beautiful again, and he had a plan to meet all of the needs for the repair of the wall.

In the third chapter, we learn some important strategies for accomplishing great things. What is it in your life that needs repair? Is there something broken? Now is the time to tap into the great plans that God has for you.

Facing the daily
challenges (Chapter 6)

In Nehemiah 4:1, we see that Nehemiah was misunderstood and ridiculed.

How do you handle ridicule?

When you are misunderstood how does that affect you?

How do you respond to these and other challenges?

Nehemiah 2:20, "The God of heaven will give us success."
Remember, Nehemiah's focus from the very beginning of the rebuilding process was on God.

Is getting and keeping a focus on God difficult for you?

What are the distractions that challenge you?

Another challenge arose during the rebuilding of the wall. In Nehemiah 4:6, we learned that the people had finished only half of their work, and then in verse ten we discovered that the people became discouraged.

What keeps you from feeling overwhelmed when you have a big task to accomplish?

Nehemiah's response was one of faith as he prayed in Nehemiah 4:9. His focus remained on God; however, in this verse we learned an additional aspect of prayer. We learned that Nehemiah watched and prayed, "But we prayed to our God and posted a guard day and night to meet this threat."

Has discouragement affected your faith? (James 1:2–4)

What do you need to be watchful for or alert to?

Nehemiah didn't retaliate; however, he and the people did protect themselves. Read Nehemiah 4:13–23, where the people moved forward with a sword in one hand and a trowel in the other.

Can you visualize this scene? The idea here is that you need to be equipped for a spiritual battle while you are going through your rebuilding process. The scriptures tell us in Ephesians 6:12, "For our struggle is not against flesh and blood, but against the rulers, against the authorities, against the powers of this dark world and against the spiritual forces of evil in the heavenly realms."

Are you familiar with the verses that follow in Ephesians 6:13–18, where believers are instructed to put on the "full armor of God"? If so, how are you applying this principle in your life?

Audio Message eight: "Facing Obstacles"
www.nehemiahresponse.com/audio/eight.asp
About the audio message: Obstacles are something that you can expect to encounter once you are resolved to start the rebuilding process for the glory of God. Obstacles can come in the form of difficulties, opposition, trials, problems, struggles, troubles, or hurdles. No matter what term you may use to identify obstacles, you can count on them happening. The major problem with obstacles is that they threaten advancement.

In the fourth chapter of Nehemiah, there are three obstacles that the people are faced with. With each obstacle Nehemiah exhibited excellent leadership skills by providing solutions. We can benefit from learning what each obstacle was and how it was solved.

Beginning to stand strong again (Chapter 7)

What does the Golden Rule say to you?

You may be able to list people or events that have hurt you. Are there any hurts to others that you have caused?

If so, is there something that you can do about it?

Read Philippians 2:3–5, and think about what you can do about following Christ's example of considering others.

What can we learn from Nehemiah about servant leadership? Compare these passages: Nehemiah 5:14–19 and 1 Peter 5:2–3.

Audio Message nine: "Getting Along with My Neighbor"
www.nehemiahresponse.com/audio/nine.asp

About the audio message: Even while working on a project centered in the will of God, people get tired. The work takes its toll. When we're tired patience can run thin, and turmoil can arise in the best of relationships. Relationships once happy, now grate on each other.

There's another dynamic during a time of weariness; it's when someone takes advantage of the situation to get ahead. The problem with this is opportunist step over others to move forward. Why do people do this? How can we keep from falling into this trap? What do we do when someone takes advantage of us?

In the fifth chapter of Nehemiah, internal strife is taking place and the day-to-day of the work is the cause. Interestingly, we see internal strife following on the heels of the outside opposition found in chapter four. Is there something to learn from such a sequence? In this message see what you can discover about this phase of Nehemiah's rebuilding process.

How do you keep on track and finish? (Chapter 8)

How consistent are you at finishing a project?

What goals have you set in the past but have never finished?

Why didn't you finish?

What seems to get in the way or what is your temptation to end early?

Notice how often they came to Nehemiah. "Four times they sent me the same message, and each time I gave them the same answer" (6:4).

Do you find that you give in when there is repeated pressure?

What are the possible temptations to stop short of finishing?

Nehemiah was faced with three distractions. They were each aimed at him. He was the leader, and if he stopped, the entire rebuilding project would stop. Following, each of the three distractions are listed. Take time to think them through and make application where it is relevant for you.

Distraction number one was the enticement of something better or different in Nehemiah 6:1–4.

How did he overcome?

He had a strong sense of what he was to be doing! He had an overriding *yes*, so it was easier to say *no*. "I am carrying on a great project and cannot go down" (6:3).

Distraction number two was the use of rumors against Nehemiah in 6:5–9.

How did he overcome the rumors?

He spoke a brief statement against the rumor and prayed to God for strength! "I sent him this reply: 'Nothing like what you are saying is happening; you are just making it up out of your head'" (6:8). " ... but I prayed, 'Now strengthen my hands'" (6:9).

Distraction number three was the use of intimidation in Nehemiah 6:10–14.

How did he overcome intimidation?

Nehemiah was evidently keenly sensitive and discerning; he says, "I realized that God had not sent him, but that he had prophesied against me because Tobiah and Sanballat had hired him" (6:12). Nehemiah also had integrity knowing and doing what is right. He was being tricked to protect himself by breaking a law. "He had been hired to intimidate me so that I would commit a sin by doing this, and then they would give me a bad name to discredit me" (6:13).

Audio Message ten: "Staying on Task"
    www.nehemiahresponse.com/audio/ten.asp
    About the audio message: From Nehemiah, we learn that in life there will be a time of rebuilding, and that rebuilding can be a battle. As we can see from chapters four through six, the rebuilding of the wall in Jerusalem met many challenges. In chapter six, the threat was

toward leadership and Nehemiah was tempted to end the project before it was finished.

Three possible distractions were posed to Nehemiah. Each one was different, and each distraction had a solution. It's interesting to learn from Nehemiah's response to each temptation.

What causes a person to get off task? What can we learn from the distractions that Nehemiah had to face and the way he handled each one?

What's so important about a time to celebrate? (Chapter 9)

How good are you at taking time to celebrate?

If you find yourself going from project to project with no break for celebration, try to understand why work dominates.

What might the integration of celebration into your life mean?

The joyous celebration in the book of Nehemiah followed a time of being in the Word. On a scale of one to ten, with ten being high, what would your number be right now for your time in the Word?

Has the work of rebuilding pulled your attention away from spiritual things?

Maintaining a balance in our lives when working on a project is of the utmost importance. Begin to identify what you value and what is important to you. If it's five or six things, visualize them hanging from a child's mobile.

What is hanging from the mobile?

If the entire mobile represents your life, are the important parts balanced the way you would like them to be?

Audio Message eleven: "What do you do when you get there?"

www.nehemiahresponse.com/audio/eleven.asp

About the audio message: Beginning in chapter seven, Nehemiah helps the people to transition from the rebuilding phase to a maintaining phase. The rebuilding of the wall is done! The workers have achieved their goal and this is a critical time, so what's next? They have gotten to where they were going, but now they could face a possible letdown … or they could sit back resting on past accomplishments … or they could sporadically move out with no specific direction in mind. If the rebuilding of the wall was not the end but a means to the end, what do you do when you get to where you are going?

Nehemiah himself transitioned into how he handled this new phase. He moved from a role of leader to administrator and launched three sequential initiatives. This message takes a look at those three initiatives and how they might apply to us.

What kind of people should we be now? (Chapter 10)

All of Israel took time to *count their blessings* in Nehemiah chapter nine. Review those in the following verses (9:7–8, 10–11, 13, 17), and let it help jog your memory of blessings.

Now make your list.

What is your response to your personal blessing list?

From chapter ten in Nehemiah Response, we learned that God is committed to us. How can you mirror God's commitment to you, back to him?

Our commitment to God and being the kind of person we should be now is expressed in four words that begin with the letter *g* in this chapter *go—grow—gather—give.*

Review the *g*'s in the chapter, and make a few notes about how God is speaking to you about each one:

Go:

Grow:

Gather:

Give:

To make these and other commitments that God puts on our heart requires change. How do you feel about change?

Is change easy or is it something of a challenge for you?

If change is hard for you, do you know why?

Is there something that you should be changing?

If so, how are you going to do it?

Audio Message twelve: "What kind of person should we be now?"

www.nehemiahresponse.com/audio/twelve.asp

About the audio message: We come to an important matter that must be faced at the end of a project. The goal has been reached; what now? We've worked hard and have gotten to where we are going, so what kind of person should we be? How has our experience changed us? What are the things that matter most? Now with the wall rebuilt, it was time for the people to look in the mirror and deep into their heart.

Remember that this was a generation whose fathers and mothers were taken captive. Serving God and living for him was something new. They rose to the occasion to rebuild the wall. It was now time for them to rethink things, asking some important questions, to help them move forward.

God had done so much for them! What was their response to be in turn? What does God expect now? The people in Nehemiah's day may have wondered, *We were born in captivity, we're now free, what should life be like?* Does all that we have gone through have purpose? Can our disaster turn out to be a blessing? Does God have plans for me beyond what we were able to see during the crisis? These exciting chapters in Nehemiah help us to know what kind of person we should be now.

Where do we go from here? (Chapter 11)

Have you ever asked yourself this question: "Could my disaster turn out to be a blessing?"

Following your rebuilding, what's next?

Was your rebuilding process the end, or was it a means to an end?

What plans do you think God might have for you?

What might be some opportunities that arise out of your rebuilding process?

Take some time to meditate on this passage. "Praise be to the God and Father of our Lord Jesus Christ, the Father of compassion and the God of all comfort, who comforts us in all our troubles, so that we can comfort those in any trouble with the comfort we ourselves have received from God" 2 Corinthians 1:3–4.

How could your crisis and rebuilding experiences be a help to others?

So, where do you go from here?

Write Your Katrina Story

If you experienced Hurricane Katrina either as a resident of the Gulf Coast or a volunteer who came to help, the following blank pages are for you to record your personal story. If you'd like to share your story with me, I'd love to hear it. You can E-mail it to me at nelson@ nehemiahresponse.com.

_____

_____

_____

_____

_____

_____

Bibliography

1   "WLOX ABC 13" Katrina, South Mississippi's Story. 2 DVD Set

2   "From Wikipedia, the free encyclopedia." Hurricane Katrina. http://en.wikipedia.org/wiki/Hurricane_Katrina

3   "The Barna Group." 2006. *Five Years Later: The 9/11 Attacks Show No Lasting Influence On Americans' Faith.* 28 August 2006 http://www.barna.org/

4   Barna Group

5   Barna Group

6   "SunHerald." Our Tsunami. 30 August 205. VOL. 121, NO. 331

7   Richard Foster, *Freedom of Simplicity* (Harper & Row, Publishers, Inc., 1981) p. 91.

8   Spencer Johnson, *Who Moved My Cheese?* (G. P. Putnam's Sons, 1998) p. 48.

9   Russell H. Conwell, *Acres of Diamonds*, http://www.britannica.com/ EBchecked/topic/ 4115/ Acres-of-Diamonds

10   Richard Exley, *The Rhythm of Life* (Honor Books, 1987) p. 107.

11   Biloxi Lighthouse to shine from US postage stamp, http://www.stampnews.com/stamps/stamps_2009/stamp_1231532839_96559.html

12   The Friendship Oak Tree, http://www.usm.edu/ gc/friendship_oak.html

13   "God of This City." Lyrics by Passion Worship Band. http://www.newreleasetuesday.com/lyrics-detail.php?lyrics_id=28083